F

G000292882

Memories of my childhood in the early nineteen sixties are firmly linked with the delicious buns my Aunt Eva, my mother's sister, baked in the Remoska. I remember lifting the lid to see if 'they were done…'

Now, many years later it is a very pleasant surprise to me to find that this is not just a 'pan' to be bought anywhere but a true Czech invention now universally discovered and thanks to Lakeland used with great success by thousands of people in Great Britain.

H E Jan Winkler
Ambassador of the Czech Republic
London 2007

Contents

Introduction

Milena Grenfell-Baines
As far back as the 1950's, Milena developed an interest in food when employed as a governess to a family in France. Acquiring a taste for French food was no hardship and learning much from the family cook was a beginning.

Working as an interpreter for three years on cookery holidays, establishing two new cookery schools in France, and promoting specialist cookery weekends across the UK was excellent experience for future activities.

Milena, together with Joan Whittle, an experienced cook, close friend and colleague, organised annual French, Austrian and Mediterranean cookery weeks in her home town of Preston, which were featured on Granada TV.

In the early 1980s, Milena together with Joan, broadcast a weekly cookery programme on Red Rose Radio in Preston.

Together with colleague Derek Smith, one time head of a catering college, now owner of his own catering company, 'Hooray for Home Cooking' has been established to promote the Remoska and its use. Introducing the Remoska to the British public has resulted in another career, when most people are well and truly retired.

Milena has maintained her interest in classical music for the past 30 years, has a close involvement with the Royal Liverpool Philharmonic Orchestra and is Chairman of the Friends of the Orchestra. Milena plans and takes Friends of the Phil on tours to the Czech Republic. Visiting conductors and soloists of the Royal Liverpool Philharmonic Orchestra are frequent guests and are catered for in the family home.

As a Czech national, she escaped to the UK as a child refugee from the Nazis in 1939, one of the 700 Jewish children saved by Sir Nicholas Winton. Her war years were spent in the Czechoslovak State Secondary School in Exile situated in Wales, and Milena still meets with her old schoolfriends at regular intervals.

In 2001 Milena was presented with the Jan Masaryk 'Gratis Agit' award, by the Czech Minister of Foreign Affairs for remaining a faithful patriot, an ambassador of goodwill, culture and history of the Czech Republic.

Widow of architect Professor Sir George Grenfell-Baines, founder of the international practice of architects, designers and engineers, Building Design Partnership (BDP), Milena has 4 children and 9 grandchildren.

Milena is grateful to her good friends and colleagues who have contributed to the recipes and production of this cookbook.

Derek Smith

As Chairman of Hooray for Home Cooking, Derek, together with Milena was responsible for bringing the Remoska to the British public. He has extensively tested and used the Remoska. He has provided several recipes for your enjoyment.

He runs his own corporate catering business for clients as diverse as local authorities, industrialists, high street banks and building societies. He has worked at many prestigious events such as the British Open Golf Championship, the Ryder Cup, Royal Show at Stoneleigh and the Commonwealth Games.

Derek served an apprenticeship as a baker and confectioner before joining the Royal Air Force as a chef. After leaving the RAF, Derek was fortunate to work with the celebrated European chef, Karl Loderer. With continual training and experience Derek started his own bakery and confectionery business, before being appointed Senior Lecturer and Head of the School of Catering at a northwest college.

He has been a Justice of the Peace for over twenty years and is Chairman of both Heartbeat Trustees Committee and Preston Town Twinning Partnership. Derek is married to Collette and has three grown-up children.

Joan Whittle

Founded on her interest in the food and cookery of different countries and cultures, Joan has spent most of her working life involved with commercial catering, as an hotelier, broadcaster and consultant. She has cooked, tested and provided recipes and acted as food consultant to this cookbook.

For several years she and Milena ran a successful catering company serving both private and corporate clients.

For seventeen years Joan presented the food programme on Lancashire's local radio station, for which in 1990 she received a Silver Heart from the Variety Club of Great Britain as Independent Broadcaster of the Year. During this time she was actively involved in running a country house hotel, and then worked on various county magazines promoting food events and recipes, and as a judge for regional food awards.

In recent years she has consulted on food development and marketing to a variety of restaurants, bistros and airlines.

continued

Jill Wadeson
Helping us to introduce the Remoska to the UK, working with the factory and the various legislative authorities; like all the contributors to this cookbook, Jill has tested recipes and cooks regularly with her Remoska. Jill has been responsible for compiling, editing and has been very closely involved with its production.

Jill is Company Secretary to Hooray for Home Cooking, responsible for the administration of the company. She had been employed as personal secretary to the founder, Sir George Grenfell-Baines and senior partners of the international firm BDP and previously, one of the directors at the former Leyland Motors Group.

Jill attended school in Switzerland, secretarial college in London, has been a Justice of the Peace and involved in charity fund raising for a number of years. She is married to Tony and has three grown-up children.

The Hooray for Home Cooking team that helped introduce the Remoska to the United Kingdom and who produced this cookbook. Standing, Derek Smith, Jill Wadeson, Joan Whittle and sitting, Milena Grenfell-Baines.

Hooray for Home Cooking would like to acknowledge and thank Lakeland for their kind assistance and co-operation in the production of this book, especially –

Matthew Canwell
Elaine Dawson
Rachel Halliday
Stephanie Mansfield
Philippa Simons

We thank Fourninety for the photographs.

All about the Remoska

'It's the lid that does the cooking'.

There is no doubt that here in the UK, as elsewhere, today's modern ovens and microwaves, ready to cook meals, takeaways and frozen food has changed our attitude to cooking. It is difficult to believe that after all the available computerised gadgetry this simple electric mini-oven, the Remoska, invented in Czechoslovakia just before World War 2 was about to make a comeback, but – simplicity – is exactly the reason for its appeal.

It was manufactured quite extensively during the 40 years of Communist rule – it was cheap, efficient and often replaced the oven in people's small kitchens.

Once liberated from the oppressive Communist regime, modern electric cookery aids available to Western Europe were being imported and the Remoska was relegated to a dark corner of some kitchen cupboard.

However, people with country cottages, caravans and small town flats were slowly reminded that here was an electric mini-oven in which mother and grandmother cooked very tasty dishes, had extolled its economic use of electricity and slowly the Remoska was once more in demand. Though the factory was still in production it was, through lack of investment, rundown and for sale.

In 1990, the factory moved to eastern Moravia where employment was needed and production began once again, mainly for the Czech market.

"On a trip to Prague, I was visiting my cousin Helen, and before leaving, I bought her, as a parting present, a new Remoska to replace the one Helen's mother had been using for the past 40 years.

Back in England, re-reading the promotional literature I was prompted to phone the factory and asked why the Remoska had never been exported abroad. Speaking to a complete stranger, before any names were given, the reply came, "paní, vy jste andel z nebe", we were speaking in Czech. Mr Ivo Svoboda, the Marketing Manager, for that is who it was, said – "lady, are you an angel from heaven…"

From that delightful encounter has grown a firm friendship. When I showed the Remoska to the Customer Director of Lakeland, the reply was *"Let me take one home, I'll have a play with it".*

Now, the Remoska has become one of Lakeland's best sellers and so many Remoskas have been sold that it was time to produce a full colour recipe book that would help you get the best from it.

Milena Grenfell-Baines

What is a Remoska?

If you've bought this book, you probably already own a Remoska!

It is an electric mini-oven with a 'lid that does the cooking'. Apart from the lid it consists of a Teflon$^{®}$ lined pan and a stand. A shallow pan is also available and recommended. The Remoska now comes in three sizes, Baby, Standard and Grand. **The recipes in this book can be cooked using either the Standard or the Grand.** The Remoska has a simple on/off switch, no graded heat control and yet it cooks just like, if not better than an oven and is amazingly economical with your electricity.

The Remoska is not a 'slow cooker'. On the contrary, some food will cook faster than in a normal oven. Each time you take the lid off you remove the source of the heat, so don't be tempted to take the lid off until you see through the glass window that the cooking is done or the right colour achieved.

Notes to the recipes

Cooking times
Times given in the recipes are as a guideline only.

Remember cooking in the Remoska is not an exact science. Times for cooking will vary depending on the contents i.e how thick your meat is and how finely you chop other ingredients.

Ingredients – no amounts
You may find in some of the recipes a quantity is not provided. This is because there is flexibility to use an amount to suit your own personal taste.

Ingredients – your choice
In some recipes, some ingredients can be of your own choice. For instance, cooking with oil, sugar, cheese, herbs, honey or breadcrumbs in particular will be ingredients that you personally prefer – using white or brown breadcrumbs will not adversely alter the recipe and will suit your taste.

Ingredients – size and weight
You will find recipes for poultry etc where only the quantity is specified. The size or weight is not quantified. This particularly applies to chicken breast, legs and thighs. It is also true for duck and other game and poultry. These items are packaged in different ways and not always sold by size or weight. Therefore buy the normal size or weight suitable for the appetites you are feeding. The variation is insuffecient to affect the recipe but do adjust cooking times accordingly.

Flour
Unless otherwise specified, flour is plain.

Paprika
In a number of the meat recipes you will find caraway seed, marjoram and paprika, all very popular ingredients in Eastern Europe. A word about paprika. There is sweet paprika and 'sharp' paprika. Our advice is to use the sweet.

Seasoning – salt and black pepper
All cooking is about personal taste, and in particular the use of seasoning is very much how you like your food. We include salt and black pepper in the list of ingredients but the amount you use is very much down to your taste. Do not forget that some ingredients, like Feta cheese, can be quite salty and may affect the amount you choose to use.

Larding
This means that you make incisions into the meat with a sharp knife, about a centimetre across and 2–3 centimetres deep and insert strips of bacon (usually fatty) about the thickness of your little finger.

Foil lids
Our experience has demonstrated that sometimes the Remoska can be too efficient and with some recipes the cooking times need extending. To ensure the top of the contents do not burn, we recommend creating a foil lid and laying this over the contents during cooking. Simply create a 'cover' by using four or five pieces of aluminium foil to fit in the Remoska and place on top of the contents.

The Remoska cooks in its own unique way.

You can bake, grill, fry, poach and roast in a Remoska, as these are common terms used in cooking. Throughout this cookbook we refer simply to 'cooking', although the end results are similar to many of the conventional cooking techniques with which you are familiar.

Frying
You can fry onions and garlic etc in the Remoska but it takes a little longer than using a frying pan. Some of these recipes therefore suggest using a frying pan to prepare some ingredients.

Baking
Cakes may be baked directly in the Remoska. Alternatively you can line with foil or use a loose-based cake tin.

You can also use Magic Non-Stick Liner (Lakeland Catalogue Ref 5570) directly in the base of the Remoska to prevent it from scratching the non-stick base.

When baking cakes, because the edges will bake slightly quicker than the centre, cut a disc of foil or the Magic Non-Stick Liner about the same diameter as the pan, then cut a hole in the centre about the diameter of a coffee mug. Place this disc over the cake for the last 15 minutes.

A message from the publisher

We would love to hear from you.

If you have any comments, thoughts or new recipes you would like to share, contact us on our websites –

http://www.hoorayforhomecooking.co.uk
http://www.remoska.co.uk

where you'll find other recipes, tips and discussion pages

General Tips

The Remoska works just like an oven. You can also make toasted sandwiches, or cook ready meals in foil containers.

Food, including cakes may be cooked from cold.

You may place your food directly in the Remoska pan or in ovenproof dishes to fit inside the Remoska pan, ensuring they are clear of the lid.

The Remoska may be used as a 'Bain Marie', heating food, defrosting food and it probably cooks the best roast chicken you have ever tasted.

Wrap portions of food in very lightly greased foil, ideal if you are on a fat free diet – fish particularly remains moist and full of flavour.

It is possible to prepare a whole meal for the family in the Remoska.

Puff pastry rises like a dream and sponge cakes stay moist.

The Remoska is extremely economical to use, easy to clean – the Teflon base is non-stick so will rinse out – not even worth putting in the dishwasher though it's quite safe to do so.

To clean the lid, switch off, unplug from the mains and when cool wipe the glass with a damp cloth.

If you need to remove the lid to stir, place it away from you upside down, **remember, it is the lid that does the cooking – it will be hot.**

When in use, the Remoska will be hot, avoid contact and keep away from plastic or flammable materials.

Do not heat the empty Remoska as with all Teflon$^{®}$ lined cooking pans, excess heating of an empty pan will damage the lining.

Never immerse the lid in water.

Keep away from children.

SOUP

There is nothing like the
homeliness and comfort
of real soup.

BAKED BEAN SOUP

	Standard		Grand	
Serves	*4–6*		*6–8*	
Oil	2 tbsp		4 tbsp	
Onion, finely sliced	1 medium		1 large	
Breadcrumbs, white, fresh	4 tbsp		8 tbsp	
Baked beans, tin	1 x 420g		2 x 420g	
Stock, chicken, hot	900ml	1¹/₂pints	1.8l	3pints
Worcestershire sauce	1 tsp		2 tsp	
Salt and black pepper				

Put the oil and onion into the Remoska and cook until the onion is soft. Add the breadcrumbs, baked beans, stock, Worcestershire sauce and season to taste, using more black pepper than salt. Cook for approx 25–30 minutes until piping hot.

Timing is the same for the Standard and Grand.

HAM & COURGETTE SOUP

	Standard		Grand	
Serves	*4*		*6–8*	
Courgettes, finely diced	225g	8oz	500g	1lb
Stock, chicken, hot	900ml	1¹/₂pints	1.5l	2¹/₄pints
Ham, lean, cooked, cut into thin strips	50g	2oz	100g	4oz
Chilli powder	¹/₂ tsp		1 tsp	
Soy sauce, light	1¹/₂ tbsp		3 tbsp	

Place all the ingredients into the Remoska and cook for 35–40 minutes or until the courgettes are soft.

Timing is the same for the Standard and Grand.

Carrot and Ginger Soup

CARROT & GINGER SOUP

	Standard		Grand	
Serves	*4*		*6–8*	
Oil	2 tbsp		3 tbsp	
Onion, finely sliced	1 large		2 large	
Garlic clove, crushed	2 cloves		3 cloves	
Curry powder	1–2 tsp		2–4 tsp	
Ginger, fresh, grated	1 tbsp		1–2 tbsp	
Carrots, peeled and diced	500g	1lb	700g	1¹/₂lb
Stock, chicken, hot	1l	32fl oz	1.5l	2¹/₄pints
Salt and black pepper				
Cream or crème fraîche	to serve		to serve	
Parsley, fresh, chopped	1 tbsp		2 tbsp	

Put the oil, onions, garlic and curry powder into the Remoska, mix lightly. Cook for approx 20 minutes or until the onions are soft and golden. Add the ginger, carrots and stock. Cook for approx 40 minutes or until the carrots are soft. Switch off the heat and leave for 10 minutes. Blitz the soup with a blender until smooth, season and serve with the addition of some cream or crème fraîche and serve with chopped parsley. For a smoother soup use the back of a ladle to pass it through a sieve into a clean bowl.

Timing is the same for the Standard and Grand.

LEEK & POTATO SOUP

	Standard		Grand	
Serves	*4–6*		*6–8*	
Butter	25g	1oz	50g	2 oz
Onion, finely sliced	1 large		2 large	
Garlic clove, crushed	1		2	
Leek, finely sliced	1 medium		1 large	
Potato, diced	175g	6oz	350g	12oz
Stock, chicken, hot	450ml	15fl oz	900ml	1 1/2pints
Salt and black pepper				
Cream, single	4 tbsp		6–8 tbsp	
Chives, fresh, chopped	1 tbsp		2 tbsp	

Put the butter, onion, garlic, leek, potatoes and stock into the Remoska and cook for approx 30–40 minutes or until the potatoes are soft. Switch off and leave for 10 minutes. Liquidise the soup until smooth and pass through a sieve into a bowl. Season to taste. Reheat in the Remoska, add the cream and serve sprinkled with the chives.

Timing is the same for the Standard and Grand.

POTATO SOUP BRAMBORACKA

	Standard		Grand	
Serves	*4–6*		*6–8*	
Butter	1 tbsp		2 tbsp	
Onion, finely sliced	1 small		1 medium	
Celery sticks, finely sliced	1		3	
Carrots, finely diced	1 medium		2 medium	
Mushrooms, chopped	2 tbsp		3 tbsp	
Garlic cloves, crushed	1		3	
Caraway seeds	1 tsp		2 tsp	
Stock, beef, hot	450ml	15fl oz	900ml	1 1/2pints
Potatoes, peeled and diced	350g	12oz	700g	1 1/2lb
Marjoram, dried	2 tsp		1 tbsp	
Garlic clove, sliced	1		1	
Salt and black pepper				
Parsley, or chives, fresh, chopped	1 tbsp		2 tbsp	

Put the butter, onion, celery, carrots, mushrooms, garlic and caraway seeds into the Remoska and cook for 25 minutes. Add the stock, potatoes and marjoram and cook for approx 40 minutes or until the potatoes are cooked. Take out one third of the soup and liquidise with the raw clove of garlic. Return to the rest of the soup, stir and check the seasoning. Sprinkle with parsley or chives and serve.

Timing is the same for the Standard and Grand.

Pea with Mint Soup

PEA WITH MINT SOUP

	Standard		Grand	
Serves	*4*		*8*	
Butter	25g	1oz	50g	2oz
Onion, finely sliced	1 medium		1 large	
Peas, frozen	500g	1lb	1kg	2lb
Stock, chicken, hot	600ml	20fl oz	1l	32fl oz
Mint jelly	2 tsp		4 tsp	
Salt and black pepper				

Put the butter and onion into the Remoska and cook until the onion is soft and golden. Add the peas, stock and mint jelly, stir, and cook for 25 minutes. Cool slightly, then liquidise and sieve, pushing through as much of the pea purée as you can. Taste, and season if necessary. Reheat.

Timing is the same for the Standard and Grand.

MUSHROOM & MARSALA SOUP

	Standard		Grand	
Serves	*4–6*		*6–8*	
Butter	50g	2oz	75g	3oz
Onion, finely sliced	1 medium		1 large	
Mushrooms, finely sliced	225g	8oz	500g	1lb
Salt and black pepper				
Stock, mushroom, hot	300ml	10fl oz	600ml	20fl oz
Milk	300ml	10fl oz	600ml	20fl oz
Marsala or sherry	2 tsp		4 tsp	

Put the butter, onion and mushrooms into the Remoska, and season with black pepper only. Cook for 20 minutes. Add the stock and milk and cook for 30 minutes. Liquidise until smooth, add the Marsala or sherry, taste and if necessary add a little salt and more black pepper.

Timing is the same for the Standard and Grand

Mushroom and Marsala Soup

Sweetcorn Soup

SWEETCORN SOUP

	Standard		Grand	
Serves	*4*		*6–8*	
Butter	2 tbsp		4 tbsp	
Spring onions, finely sliced	1 bunch		2 bunches	
Sweetcorn, tin, drained	1 x 320g		2 x 320g	
Milk	750ml	25fl oz	1.5l	2^1/$_4$pints
Nutmeg, fresh, grated	^{1}/$_4$ tsp		^{1}/$_2$ tsp	
Salt and black pepper				
Chives, fresh, chopped	1 tbsp		4 tbsp	

Put the butter and spring onions into the Remoska and cook until the onions are soft but not brown. Add the sweetcorn, milk, nutmeg and season to taste, (use more black pepper than salt). Cook for approx 40–45 minutes. Liquidise, pass the soup through a sieve. Adjust the seasoning if necessary, sprinkle with chives and serve.

Timing is the same for the Standard and Grand.

VEGET

ABLES

Most vegetables are excellent when roasted in the Remoska. Simply clean and peel, add a light coating of oil, season and cook!

AUBERGINE SOUFFLÉ

	Standard		Grand	
Serves	*4*		*8*	
Aubergine	2		4	
Béchamel sauce	250ml	8fl oz	600ml	20fl oz
Eggs	4		7	
Cheese, grated	175g	6oz	350g	12oz
Breadcrumbs, fresh	2 tbsp		3–4 tbsp	

Slice the aubergines in half lengthwise, place cut side down on an oiled baking sheet and bake in a very hot oven 230C/450F/Gas 8 for approx 20 minutes. Remove the skin and mash the pulp. While the aubergines are baking make the Béchamel sauce (see page 180). Separate the eggs and whisk up the whites stiffly. Combine the aubergine pulp, the Béchamel sauce, half the cheese and the egg yolks. Fold in the stiffly beaten egg whites. Grease the Remoska and coat with the breadcrumbs – this helps the mixture to 'climb'. Pour the mixture into the Remoska, sprinkle with the rest of the cheese. Bake for approx 40–50 minutes until well risen and golden. Serve immediately.

Timing is the same for the Standard and Grand.

CABBAGE GOULASH

	Standard		Grand	
Serves	*4–6*		*6–8*	
Butter	25g	1oz	50g	2oz
Cabbage, finely sliced	1 small		1 medium	
Stock, chicken, hot	300ml	10fl oz	600ml	20fl oz
Salt and black pepper				
Tomato purée	1 tbsp		2 tbsp	
Paprika, sweet	1/2–1 tsp		1–11/2 tsp	
Bratwurst or Frankfurters	3–4		4–6	

Place the butter, cabbage and hot stock into the Remoska and cook for approx 30–40 minutes or until the cabbage is soft. Add a little more hot stock if necessary. The stock should just cover the cabbage. Season, using more black pepper than salt. Liquidise a third of the mixture and return to the Remoska. Add the tomato purée, paprika and the sausages cut into thin slices. Stir, and cook for approx 10–15 minutes or until the sausages are cooked.

Timing is the same for the Standard and Grand.

ROASTED ASPARAGUS

	Standard	Grand
Serves	*4*	*8–10*
Asparagus, fresh	to suit	to suit
Oil, olive		
Salt and black pepper		
Lemon, juice		
Vinegar, Balsamic		
Cheese, Parmesan		

Use the Shallow Pan.

The quantity you need depends on the size of asparagus, buy enough to cover the base of the Remoska twice. Clean and peel the stalks, trimming to the same length. Very lightly coat the asparagus with oil, turning them gently with your hands. Season with salt and freshly ground black pepper. Layer the base of the Remoska and one extra layer. Cook for approx 10–15 minutes.

Transfer to a serving dish, and drizzle with lemon juice, dash of Balsamic vinegar and shavings of Parmesan cheese.

Timing is the same for the Standard and Grand depending on the thickness of the Asparagus.

AUBERGINES WITH TOMATOES & RAISINS

	Standard		Grand	
Serves	4		6–8	
Oil, vegetable	2 tbsp		4 tbsp	
Cumin seeds	1/2 tsp		1 tsp	
Onions, finely diced	2 medium		3 medium	
Garlic purée	1 tsp		2 tsp	
Ginger, grated root	1 tsp		2 tsp	
Tikka Masala paste	1 tbsp		2 tbsp	
Raisins	50g	2oz	100g	4oz
Aubergines, peeled, diced	300g	10oz	500g	1lb
Tomatoes, chopped, tin	1 x 400g		2 x 400g	

Heat the oil in the Remoska for 10–15 minutes, and add the cumin seeds, onions, garlic purée and ginger. Cook for approx 15–20 minutes or until the onions are soft. Stir in the Tikka Masala paste, raisins, aubergines and tomatoes. Cook for approx 40–50 minutes or until the aubergines are cooked.

Timing is the same for the Standard and Grand.

BROCCOLI BAKED WITH CHEESE

	Standard		Grand	
Serves	4		8–10	
Broccoli	500g	1lb	1kg	2lb
Butter, for greasing				
Peas, frozen	200g	7oz	400g	14oz
Carrots, sliced	2 medium		4 medium	
Nutmeg, fresh, grated	to taste		to taste	
Parsley, fresh, chopped	2 tbsp		4 tbsp	
Salt and black pepper				
Béchamel sauce	250ml	8fl oz	600ml	20 fl oz
Cheese, Cheddar, grated	50g	2oz	175g	6oz

In a saucepan, cook the broccoli, break into florets and place in the greased Remoska. Add the peas, carrots, nutmeg, parsley, season and stir gently. Pour on the Béchamel sauce (see page 180), cover with the cheese and cook for approx 30–45 minutes or until the top is crisp and golden in colour.

Timing is the same for the Standard and Grand.

Aubergine, Tomato and Feta Bake

AUBERGINE, TOMATO & FETA BAKE

	Standard		Grand	
Serves	*4*		*6–8*	
Aubergine, sliced and diced	1		2	
Shallots, finely sliced	4		6	
Garlic clove, crushed	1		2	
Oil, olive	1 tbsp		2 tbsp	
Tomatoes with herbs, tin	1 x 400g		*see below	
Thyme, leaves, fresh	2 tbsp		2 tbsp	
Sugar	1/2 tsp		1 tsp	
Black pepper				
Cheese, Feta, diced	100g	4oz	175g	6oz
Breadcrumbs, fresh	50g	2oz	100g	4oz
Cheese, Cheddar, grated	50g	2oz	100g	4oz
Parsley, fresh, chopped	2 tbsp		2 tbsp	

Place the aubergine, shallots, garlic and oil into the Remoska. Cook for approx 15–25 minutes or until the aubergine is soft. Add the tomatoes, (*if using the Grand Remoska, use one and a half tins) thyme and sugar and season to taste with black pepper. Mix well. Dot with the Feta cheese and cook for 20 minutes. Mix together the breadcrumbs, cheese and parsley, sprinkle evenly over the aubergine and tomato mix and cook for approx 20–30 minutes more until the topping is golden.

Timing is the same for the Standard and Grand.

CABBAGE PIE

	Standard		Grand	
Serves	*4–6*		*8–10*	
Loose leaf cabbage	1		1	
Stuffing				
Bread, white, thick slices	2		4	
Onion, chopped	1 medium		1 large	
Oil, vegetable	1 tbsp		2 tbsp	
Garlic clove	1		2	
Egg	1 large		2 small	
Pork or lamb, minced	300g	10oz	500g	1lb
Salt and black pepper				

From the base of the cabbage cut away 8–10 (Standard) or 10–12 leaves, (Grand) place into a large saucepan of salted boiling water and cook until the thick core at the base of the leaves is soft. Drain, flatten the leaves out on a tea towel and cut away the core. Brush the base and sides of the Remoska with oil and cover the base with 4–5 (Standard) or 6–8 (Grand) cabbage leaves.

Stuffing
Moisten the bread in 2–3 tablespoons of water and squeeze the water out. In a non-stick frying pan fry the onions in the oil until soft, add the crushed garlic, switch off and cool. Stir the bread, onion, garlic and the whisked egg into the minced meat. Mix well, if it seems too dry add 1 tablespoon of water.

Add the meat stuffing to the cabbage leaves in the Remoska, cover with the rest of the cabbage leaves, brush with oil, and cook for approx 30–40 minutes.

If using the Grand cook approx 10–15 minutes longer.

STUFFED CABBAGE LEAVES

	Standard			Grand		
Serves	*4*			*8*		
Cabbage leaves	4 large			8 large		
Stuffing						
Breadcrumbs, fresh	2 tbsp			4 tbsp		
Milk	1 tbsp			2 tbsp		
Butter	50g	2oz		100g	4oz	
Onion, chopped	2 small			2 medium		
Garlic clove, crushed	1			2		
Pork, minced	200g	7oz		400g	14oz	
Beef, minced	200g	7oz		400g	14oz	
Egg	1			2		
Parsley, fresh, chopped	1 tbsp			2 tbsp		
Marjoram, dried	1 tsp			2 tsp		
Salt and black pepper						
Butter, for greasing						
Stock, vegetable, warm	200ml	7fl oz		400ml	14fl oz	
Tomatoes, chopped, tin	1 x 200g			1 x 400g		
Sugar	1 tsp			2 tsp		

In a saucepan blanch the cabbage leaves in boiling salted water for 5 minutes to soften, drain and flatten out lightly with a rolling pin.

Stuffing
Soak the breadcrumbs in the milk and squeeze dry. In a non-stick frying pan cook one of the onions in the butter, add the garlic and mix with the minced meats, bread-crumbs, egg, parsley, marjoram and season. Divide the mixture into 4 or 8 portions and roll up in the cabbage leaves, securing either with a cocktail stick or tie up with cotton.

Butter the Remoska, add the other chopped onion, the stock, tomatoes and sprinkle in the sugar. Place the cabbage rolls on top, and cook for approx 40–50 minutes basting from time to time.

Timing is the same for the Standard and Grand.

CAULIFLOWER & BROCCOLI

	Standard		Grand	
Serves	*4*		*8*	
Cauliflower	225g	8oz	500g	1lb
Broccoli	225g	8oz	500g	1lb
Coriander seeds, crushed	1 tsp		1 tbsp	
Garlic cloves	2		3	
Salt and black pepper				
Oil, olive	2 tbsp		2 tbsp	
Cheese, Mozzarella	175g	6oz	350g	12oz

Trim the cauliflower and broccoli into florets 2.5cm (1in) diameter. Place in a large mixing bowl and sprinkle with the coriander. Crush the garlic with ¾ level teaspoon of salt in a pestle and mortar until it becomes a paste. Whisk the oil into this and pour the mixture over the cauliflower and broccoli. Use your hands to toss and mix everything together to coat the vegetables well. Transfer into the Remoska and season with salt and black pepper. Cook for approx 40 minutes or until tender.

Finally sprinkle the Mozzarella over the top of the vegetables and cook for approx 10 minutes until the cheese is melted.

Timing is the same for the Standard and Grand.

CHEESE COURGETTES

	Standard		Grand	
Serves	*4–6*		*8–10*	
Courgettes, halved	2 large		3 large	
Oil for greasing				
Cheese, grated	50g	2oz	100g	4oz
Egg, hardboiled, chopped	1		2	
Ham, cooked, chopped	50g	2oz	100g	4oz
Parsley, fresh, chopped	1 tbsp		2 tbsp	
Salt and black pepper				

Scoop out the centres of the courgettes and arrange the shells in the lightly oiled Remoska. Mix the scooped out flesh with half the cheese, the egg, ham, parsley and season to taste. Spoon into the courgette shells and sprinkle with the rest of the cheese. Cook for approx 25–30 minutes or until golden brown.

Timing is the same for the Standard and Grand.

COURGETTES IN PASSATA

	Standard		Grand	
Serves	*4*		*8*	
Courgettes, thinly sliced	3 large		6 large	
Onion, red, sliced	1 small		2 small	
Garlic clove, crushed	1		2	
Passata	250ml	8fl oz	600ml	20fl oz
Thyme, fresh, chopped	2 tbsp		4 tbsp	
Salt and black pepper				
Thyme, fresh, sprigs				

Arrange half the courgettes, onion and garlic in the Remoska. Spoon half the passata over the vegetables and sprinkle with some of the chopped thyme. Season to taste. Arrange the remaining courgettes, onion and garlic in the Remoska on top of the passata and season. Spoon over the remaining passata and spread evenly.

Cook for approx 40 minutes, or until the courgettes are tender. Garnish with sprigs of thyme and serve hot.

Timing is the same for the Standard and Grand.

Courgettes in Passata

SWEET & SOUR COURGETTES

	Standard		Grand	
Serves	*4*		*6–8*	
Courgettes	500g	1lb	700g	1¹/₂lb
Salt				
Oil, olive	1 tbsp		2 tbsp	
Vinegar, wine	3 tbsp		6 tbsp	
Cinnamon, ground	¹/₂ tsp		1 tsp	
Sugar	2 tbsp		3 tbsp	
Sultanas	50g	2oz	75g	3oz
Black pepper				

Wash, top and tail the courgettes then cut into diagonal slices and place into a colander, lightly salting each layer. Leave for 30 minutes. Put the oil into the Remoska and heat for 10 minutes. Drain the courgettes, then pat dry with kitchen paper and add to the Remoska. Cook for approx 20 minutes. Add the vinegar, cinnamon, sugar and sultanas and plenty of freshly ground black pepper and mix lightly. Cook for a further 10 minutes. Switch off the heat and leave the lid on for 15 minutes. Serve hot or cold.

Timing is the same for the Standard and Grand.

FENNEL AU GRATIN

	Standard		Grand	
Serves	*4*		*8*	
Fennel bulbs	2		4	
Salt and black pepper				
Nutmeg, fresh, grated				
Cheese, Parmesan, grated	50g	2oz	125g	5oz
Butter	50g	2oz	100g	4oz

Wash the fennel bulbs, removing any discoloured leaves, trim and halve. Cook in a saucepan in lightly salted water until tender for approx 25–30 minutes. Drain well and place into the Remoska cut side uppermost. Sprinkle with salt, pepper and nutmeg. Cover with the Parmesan cheese and dot with little pieces of butter. Cook for approx 30 minutes until just browned.

Timing is the same for the Standard and Grand.

FENNEL CASSEROLE

	Standard	Grand
Serves	*4*	*8*
Fennel, bulbs	3 large	6 large
Oil, olive	2 tbsp	3 tbsp
Onion, finely chopped	1 large	2 large
Garlic cloves	2	4
Tomatoes, chopped, tin	1 x 400g	2 x 400g
Salt and black pepper		
Breadcrumbs, fresh	4 tbsp	8 tbsp
Cheese, Cheddar, grated	4 tbsp	8 tbsp

Keeping some of the feathery tops for garnish, discard any coarse outer leaves of the fennel and cut out the root base. Slice the bulbs very thinly. Heat the oil in the Remoska and cook the chopped onion and garlic until soft. Add the fennel, cook for a further 15 minutes, add the tomatoes and seasoning, stir well, and cook for approx 10–15 minutes. Mix the breadcrumbs with the cheese, sprinkle over the top and cook for approx 15–20 minutes more until the top is crisp and golden. Garnish with fennel tops.

Timing is the same for the Standard and Grand.

KIDNEY BEAN BAKE

	Standard		Grand	
Serves	*4–6*		*6–8*	
Beans, red kidney, tin	1 x 410g		2 x 410g	
Carrot, finely diced	1		2	
Courgette, finely sliced	175g	6oz	300g	10oz
Water, hot	100ml	4fl oz	200ml	7fl oz
Tomato and herb sauce in a jar	1 x 500g		2 x 500g	
Cumin, ground	1 tsp		2 tsp	
Chilli powder	1/2 tsp		1 tsp	
Onion, finely chopped	1 small		1 medium	
Garlic cloves	2		3	
Salt and black pepper				

Drain the tin of red kidney beans. Place all the ingredients into the Remoska, stir and cook for approx 35 minutes. Check that the carrot and onion are cooked, if necessary adding a little more water, and continue cooking for a further approx 10–15 minutes or until they are cooked through. Season to taste. Serve hot or cold.

Timing is the same for the Standard and Grand.

LEEKS WITH BACON & POTATOES

	Standard		Grand	
Serves	*4*		*6–8*	
Oil, olive	1 tbsp		2 tbsp	
Leeks, washed, finely sliced	500g	1lb	700g	1¹/₂lb
Bacon, finely sliced	200g	7oz	350g	12oz
Potatoes, finely sliced	700g	1¹/₂lb	1kg	2lb
Stock, vegetable or chicken, hot	150ml	5fl oz	200ml	7fl oz
Black pepper				
Cheese, grated	100g	4oz	175g	6oz

Put the oil, leeks, bacon and potatoes into the Remoska and mix together. Add the stock and season to taste with black pepper. Cook for approx 45–50 minutes or until the vegetables are soft. Sprinkle the cheese over the mixture and cook for a further 15 minutes until the cheese is melted and light brown.

Timing is the same for the Standard and Grand.

LEEKS CARAMELISED WITH NOODLES

	Standard		Grand	
Serves	*2*		*4*	
Oil, olive	¹/₂ tbsp		1 tbsp	
Margarine	1 tbsp		1¹/₂ tbsp	
Leeks, large	2		4	
Sugar, dark brown soft	¹/₂ tbsp		1 tbsp	
Pasta noodles	125g	5oz	300g	10oz
Parsley, chopped	2 tbsp		3 tbsp	
Oil, olive	1 tsp		2 tsp	
Salt and black pepper				
Cheese, Parmesan, grated				

Warm the olive oil and the margarine in the Remoska. Split the leeks lengthways and wash, slice across into thin strips including the green part. When the margarine has melted, add the leeks and stir well. Cook for approx 10 minutes until the leeks start to soften. Sprinkle in the sugar, stir well and leave to cook for a further 10–15 minutes until the leeks start to caramelise.

While the leeks are cooking, cook the noodles according to the instruction on the packet and drain – keep warm.

When the leeks are done add the parsley, olive oil, cooked noodles and seasoning to taste. Toss well, top with Parmesan cheese and serve.

Leeks Baked with Ham

LEEKS BAKED WITH HAM

	Standard		Grand	
Serves	*4*		*6–8*	
Leeks	4		10	
Ham, Parma or Serrano, thin slices	4		10	
Butter	15g	1/2oz	25g	1oz
Salt and black pepper				
Parmesan, fresh, grated	2 tbsp		4 tbsp	
Cream, double	250ml	8fl oz	400ml	14fl oz
Parsley, fresh, chopped	2 tbsp		4 tbsp	
Thyme, fresh, chopped	1/2 tbsp		1 tbsp	
Rosemary, fresh, chopped	1/2 tbsp		1 tbsp	
Breadcrumbs, fresh	3 tbsp		5 tbsp	

Trim the leeks so that they are all one size. Cook the leeks in a large saucepan of salted water for 6–8 minutes. Drain and reserve about 4 tablespoons of the cooking water. Squeeze excess water out of the leeks. Wrap each leek in a slice of ham.

Lightly butter the Remoska and arrange the leeks in one layer. Season to taste with salt and black pepper and scatter half the grated Parmesan over the leeks. Mix the cream, the cooking water and the herbs, season and pour over the leeks. Sprinkle the breadcrumbs and the remaining cheese over the leeks. Cook for approx 35–40 minutes until bubbling and browned.

Timing is the same for the Standard and Grand.

MUSHROOM GOULASH

	Standard		Grand	
Serves	4		6	
Oil	2 tbsp		2 tbsp	
Onion, finely chopped	1 large		2 large	
Mushrooms, sliced	225g	8oz	350g	12oz
Garlic clove, crushed	2		2	
Paprika, sweet	1 tbsp		2 tbsp	
Cream, soured	small tub		small tub	
Milk, to thin				
Flour, plain	1 tbsp		1 tbsp	
Salt and black pepper				
Lemon juice to taste				

Heat the oil in the Remoska, add the onion and cook until transparent. Add the mushrooms and the garlic, stir and cook for approx 15–20 minutes until the mushrooms are soft. Sprinkle with paprika, stir well. Cook for approx 10–15 minutes. Add a small amount of milk to the soured cream and stir it into the flour. Add this to the mushrooms, stir and cook for approx 10–12 minutes to cook the flour and thicken the goulash. Season to taste adding lemon juice to sharpen the flavour to suit you.

Timing is the same for the Standard and Grand.

MUSHROOM TOAST TOP UP

	Standard or Grand	
Serves	4	
Garlic cloves	2	
Butter	75g	3oz
French stick, sliced	1	
Mushrooms, flat	300g	10oz
Lemon, juice	1	

Make a garlic butter by crushing the garlic cloves and creaming with half the butter. Spread each French stick slice with a small amount of the garlic butter, arrange in the Remoska and cover with open mushrooms. Dot with the remaining butter and a squeeze of lemon juice. Cook for approx 15–20 minutes until the mushrooms are cooked and the bread golden brown. Eat hot.

Timing is the same for the Standard and Grand.

MUSHROOM RISOTTO

	Standard		Grand	
Serves	*4*		*8*	
Mushrooms, Porcini, dried	15g	$^1/_2$oz	25g	1oz
Water, boiling	600ml	20fl oz	900ml	1$^1/_2$pints
Mushrooms, fresh	225g	8oz	400g	14oz
Butter	50g	2oz	100g	4oz
Onion, finely chopped	1		2	
Rice, risotto	175g	6oz	350g	12oz
Martini, sweet	150ml	5fl oz	300ml	10fl oz
Salt and black pepper				
Parmesan, grated	2 tbsp		4 tbsp	
Parmesan, shaved	50g	2oz	100g	4oz

Place the dried mushrooms in a bowl and pour the water over them. Leave to soak for half an hour, meanwhile dice the fresh mushrooms. Melt the butter in a medium sized saucepan, add the onion and cook over a gentle heat for approx 5 minutes. Add the fresh mushrooms, stir well and set aside.

Sieve the liquid from the porcini mushrooms through a double sheet of kitchen towel into a bowl and reserve. Squeeze any excess liquid out of the mushrooms and finely chop them. Add to the mushrooms and onion mixture in the saucepan and cook gently for approx 20 minutes to release the juices. Meanwhile, pour enough of the strained mushroom-soaking liquid into the Remoska to cover the base and switch on the lid to heat.

Add the rice to the mushrooms and onion mixture and stir to coat. Add the Martini and half of the remaining mushroom liquid. Add 1 level teaspoon of salt and some freshly ground black pepper and bring to simmering point. Transfer the mixture into the Remoska and stir once. Cook for exactly 20 minutes, then stir in the grated Parmesan, turning the rice grains over, and adding extra mushroom liquid to moisten if necessary. Cook for approx further 15 minutes, adding a little more liquid if necessary. Serve immediately, sprinkled with Parmesan shavings.

Although the timing is the same for Standard and Grand this recipe needs watching as risotto rice varies depending upon which brand you buy.

Milena's Tip

Mushroom stalks can be tough, especially on wild mushrooms. Remove and use in soups and stews.

STUFFED ONIONS

	Standard		Grand	
Serves	*4*		*6*	
Onions	5 medium		8 medium	
Oil, olive	1 tbsp		2 tbsp	
Allspice	$1/2$ tsp		$1/2$ tsp	
Bacon, diced	50g	2oz	100g	4oz
Pork, minced	200g	7oz	400g	14oz
Breadcrumbs, fresh	2 tbsp		4 tbsp	
Parsley, fresh, chopped	2 tbsp		3 tbsp	
Oregano, fresh, chopped	2 tsp		1 tbsp	
Cinnamon, ground	$1/2$ tsp		$1/2$ tsp	
Salt and black pepper				
Butter	25g	1oz	50g	2oz

Place the onions in a large saucepan, cover with water and bring to boil. Reduce the heat and simmer for 15–20 minutes. Drain and cool. Cut the top off, about one third down and with a sharp knife and a teaspoon hollow out the centres, leaving a shell of 2–3 layers. Stand in the Remoska. Chop the flesh removed from the onions. Heat the oil in a non-stick frying pan, cook the chopped onion over a low heat until it begins to brown. Add the allspice and cook a little longer. Remove and set aside. Fry the bacon until the fat melts, add the pork and fry until it begins to brown. In a bowl mix the breadcrumbs, pork, bacon, parsley, oregano and cinnamon. Season well and mix to form the stuffing. Fill the onions with the stuffing, dot the butter on top, and cook for 30–40 minutes until the topping is browned and crisp.

Timing is the same for the Standard and Grand.

RED CABBAGE RAGOUT

	Standard		Grand	
Serves	*4*		*8*	
Cabbage, red, finely shredded	1kg	2lb	1.5kg	3lb
Oil	1 tbsp		3 tbsp	
Onion, thinly sliced	2 large		4 large	
Apples, dessert, sliced	2		4	
Cinnamon, ground	$1/2$ tsp		1 tsp	
Caraway seeds	1 tsp		2 tsp	
Wine, white	4 tbsp		6 tbsp	
Water	4 tbsp		6 tbsp	
Salt and black pepper				

Remove any tough or wilted outside leaves from the cabbage. Heat the oil in the Remoska, stir in the onion and cook until tender. Add the apples, cinnamon and caraway and cook for approx 10 minutes. Add the cabbage, wine and water. Stir well, cover with four layers of buttered foil, and cook for approx 1–1$1/2$ hours, giving it an occasional stir. Season well and serve with sour cream. Serve hot or cold.

Timing is the same for the Standard and Grand.

Peppers Stuffed with Cous Cous and Pancetta

PEPPERS STUFFED WITH COUS COUS & PANCETTA

	Standard		Grand	
Serves	*4*		*6–8*	
Peppers, red	4 large		6–8 large	
Cous Cous, Mediterranean, packet	1 x 120g		2 x 120g	
Pancetta or streaky bacon, finely chopped	100g	4oz	175g	6oz
Mushrooms, finely chopped	100g	4oz	175g	6oz
Butter				

Cut the tops off the peppers, removing most of the stalk, and keep the tops for later. De-seed the peppers and cut a thin slice off the bottom of each pepper so that they stand upright. Make up the cous cous according to the packet and set aside. Dry fry the pancetta (or streaky bacon) until crisp. Mix together the cous cous, pancetta (or streaky bacon) and mushrooms and stuff each pepper with the mixture. Place in the Remoska, dot with butter and replace the pepper tops. Cook for approx 40–50 minutes until tender.

Timing is the same for the Standard and Grand.

Note The peppers must be no deeper than 7cm (2½in) to fit in the Remoska.

PARSNIP GRATIN

	Standard		Grand	
Serves	4		8	
Butter for greasing				
Parsnips, sliced	6 medium		12 medium	
Sausages (your choice)	500g	1lb	1kg	2lb
Black pepper				
Thyme, leaves, fresh	2 tsp		4 tsp	
Cheese sauce	600ml	20fl oz	900ml	1¹/₂pt
Cheese, Gruyère, grated	175g	6oz	350g	12oz
Breadcrumbs, fresh	3 tbsp		6 tbsp	
Butter, melted	2 tbsp		4 tbsp	

Peel and boil the parsnips until just tender. Place half of them in the buttered Remoska in as even a layer as possible. Skin the sausages and crumble into a basin adding plenty of black pepper and the thyme. Spread the sausagemeat over the parsnips and place the remaining parsnips on top. Make a cheese sauce (see page 182), stirring in half the Gruyère and pour over the parsnips. Mix the rest of the cheese with the breadcrumbs and scatter over the top. Drizzle the melted butter over the breadcrumb and cheese mix and cook for approx 35–45 minutes.

Timing is the same for the Standard and Grand.

ROASTED RED ONIONS

	Standard		Grand	
Serves	6		10–12	
Onions, red, unpeeled	6		10–12	
Tomato Butter				
Butter, softened	100g	4oz	300g	10oz
Tomatoes, sun dried in olive oil	50g	2oz	125g	5oz
Basil or parsley, fresh, chopped	2 tbsp		6 tbsp	
Salt and black pepper				
Cheese, crumbly	225g	8oz	500g	1lb
Chives, fresh, snipped				

Place the unpeeled onions in the Remoska lined with foil. Cook until the onions are tender and feel soft when squeezed, approx 1–1¹/₄ hours for both sizes of Remoska.

Tomato butter
Cream the butter, beat in the finely chopped and drained tomatoes, basil or parsley and season to taste. Shape into a roll, wrap in foil and chill. Slit the tops of the onions and open them up. Season with plenty of black pepper and add chunks of the tomato butter. Sprinkle with cheese and chives and serve immediately.

Timing is the same for the Standard and Grand.

RATATOUILLE

	Standard		Grand	
Serves	*4*		*8*	
Oil, olive	1 tbsp		3 tbsp	
Onions, peeled, quartered	175g	6oz	300g	10oz
Garlic cloves, chopped	2		4	
Aubergines, unpeeled, cubed	1		2	
Courgettes, sliced	2		4	
Peppers, red, diced	2		4	
Tomatoes	4 large		6 large	
Tomato purée	1 tbsp		3 tbsp	
Salt and black pepper				

Heat the oil in the Remoska and fry the onions and garlic until soft. Add all the other ingredients, stir and cook for approx 30–45 minutes until the vegetables are soft. Season to taste. May be served hot or cold.

Timing is the same for the Standard and Grand.

Ratatouille

SPINACH PIE

	Standard		Grand	
Serves	*4*		*8*	
Spinach, fresh	500g	1lb	1kg	2lb
Onion, chopped	1 large		2 large	
Oil, olive	1 tbsp		2 tbsp	
Garlic clove, chopped	1		2	
Mushrooms, sliced	175g	6oz	225g	8oz
Salt and black pepper				
Eggs	4		5	
Cheese, Feta	225g	8oz	350g	12oz
Cheese, Parmesan, grated	50g	2oz	100g	4oz
Parsley, fresh, chopped	2 tbsp		4 tbsp	
Oregano, fresh, chopped	1 tbsp		1 tbsp	
Butter, melted	175g	6oz	300g	10oz
Filo pastry	8 sheets		12 sheets	

Wash the spinach in plenty of cold water and place in a large saucepan. Wilt down.
(there should be enough water clinging to the leaves to cook them without adding any
extra). Tip into a colander, squeeze as dry as possible and finely chop. In a non-stick
frying pan add the oil and cook the onion, garlic and mushrooms until soft. Season to
taste. Remove from the heat. Whisk the eggs in a large bowl, crumble in the Feta, add
the Parmesan, spinach, onion and mushrooms. Stir in the parsley, oregano, salt and
freshly ground black pepper (remember the Feta is salty).

Brush the Remoska with some of the melted butter. Spread out the filo pastry. Brush
each sheet with melted butter and cover the Remoska base and sides with 4 sheets
for the Standard and 6 sheets for the Grand, allowing the pastry to overhang the edge.
Add the filling and fold the overhanging sheets of pastry over the top, buttering each
as you fold it over. Do not worry if it tears. Use up the remaining sheets of pastry
to cover the top, buttering each sheet. With the sharp point of a knife score a large
diamond pattern across the pastry and brush with butter.

Cook for 30–50 minutes until the pastry is crisp and golden, it should shrink a little
from the side of the Remoska.

Timing is the same for the Standard and Grand.

Spinach Pie

Milena's Tip

You can use a kitchen blowtorch to 'finish off' roasted
vegetables to give them that deep roasted appearance.

TOMATOES WITH BALSAMIC VINEGAR

	Standard	Grand
Serves	*4–6*	*6–8*
Tomatoes	4–6 medium	6–8 medium
Vinegar, Balsamic	2 tbsp	4 tbsp
Oil, olive	2 tbsp	4 tbsp
Sugar, caster	1/2 tbsp	1 tbsp
Salt and black pepper		

Cut the tomatoes in half and place cut side up in the Remoska. Drizzle the vinegar and oil over the tomatoes, then sprinkle with the sugar and season. Cook for approx 20–25 minutes.

Timing is the same for the Standard and Grand.

SWEETCORN & RED PEPPER FRITTERS

	Standard or Grand	
Serves	*4–6*	
Makes approx 12 fritters		

Sweetcorn, tin	1 x 320g	
Pepper, red, finely chopped	1	
Eggs, separated	3	
Breadcrumbs, white, fresh	6 tbsp	
Potato, instant	2 tbsp	
Baking powder	1 tsp	
Salt and black pepper		
Oil	2–3 tbsp	

Drain the sweetcorn and add the red pepper. Whisk the yolks and add to the corn mix. Whisk the egg whites until stiff, fold in, add the breadcrumbs, instant potato, the baking powder and the seasoning. Mix together and divide into about 12 pieces. Shape into small, thick and flattened pancakes. Heat the oil in the Remoska and cook the pancakes on both sides until brown.

Timing is the same for the Standard and Grand.

TOMATO SOUFFLÉS

	Standard		Grand	
Serves	*4*		*8*	
Tomatoes, beef	4 large		8 large	
Salt				
Milk	50ml	2fl oz	100ml	4fl oz
Cheese, Cheddar, grated	100g	4oz	200g	7oz
Garlic clove, crushed	1		2	
Eggs, separated	2		4	
Marjoram, dried	1 tsp		2 tsp	
Salt and black pepper				
Oil for greasing				

Cut the tops off the tomatoes, cut a thin slice off the bottom of each tomato so that they stand upright. Carefully scoop out the seeds and the flesh with a teaspoon, lightly salt the inside of the tomatoes and drain them upside down on a plate for 15 minutes. Meanwhile, in a saucepan, heat the milk until just warm, add most of the cheese (retaining some for a topping) the garlic, the egg yolks, marjoram and the seasoning and heat until the cheese melts and the mixture slightly thickens, stirring frequently.

Whisk the egg whites until stiff and fold into the cheese mixture. Spoon some of the mixture into each tomato shell and place the filled shells into the oiled Remoska. Sprinkle the remaining cheese on top and cook for approx 30–40 minutes and serve.

Timing is the same for Standard and Grand.

Milena's Tip

When cooking broccoli, peel the outer layer of the stems with a potato peeler or sharp knife to ensure they cook as quickly as the florets.

VEGETABLE BASKET

	Grand	
Serves	*8*	
Potatoes, peeled	1kg	2lb
Cheese, Cheddar	100g	4oz
Onion	1 large	
Oil	4 tbsp	
Leeks, finely chopped	3	
Carrots, diced	500g	1lb
Parsnips, diced	250g	9oz
Mushrooms, sliced	225g	8oz
Parsley, fresh, chopped	2 tbsp	
Salt and black pepper		
Cheese, grated	100g	4oz

Grate the raw potatoes, the cheese and half the onion into a large bowl. Stir in 2 tablespoons of the oil and mix well to combine. Press the mixture into the Remoska building up the sides to form a shell. Cook for approx 30–40 minutes until the crust begins to brown.

Meanwhile heat the remaining oil in a large non-stick frying pan and slowly fry the remaining vegetables for 5–10 minutes, adding the mushrooms for the last 5 minutes. Add 1 tablespoon of parsley and season. Place the vegetables into the potato shell, sprinkle the grated cheese mixed with the remaining parsley on top and cook for approx 20 minutes until crisp and the cheese melted.

Milena's Tip

Parsley stalks used in making stock or sauces have more flavour than the leaves.

Tomatoes Stuffed with Walnuts

TOMATOES STUFFED WITH WALNUTS

	Standard		Grand	
Serves	*4*		*8*	
Tomatoes	4 large		8 large	
Breadcrumbs, fresh	50g	2oz	125g	5oz
Walnut pieces	50g	2oz	125g	5oz
Onion, finely chopped	25g	1oz	75g	3oz
Parsley, fresh, chopped	1 tsp		1 tbsp	
Mint, fresh, chopped	1 tsp		1 tbsp	
Salt and black pepper				
Egg	1		2	
Butter	25g	1oz	50g	2oz

Cut the tops off the tomatoes. Scoop out insides and mix with the breadcrumbs, walnuts, onion and herbs. Season and bind with the egg. Stuff the tomatoes with the mixture and dot with butter. Replace the tops and cook in the Remoska for approx 25–35 minutes.

Timing is the same for the Standard and Grand.

VEGETABLE FARMHOUSE PIE

	Standard		Grand	
Serves	*4*		*8–10*	
Oil	1 tbsp		2 tbsp	
Onions, sliced	100g	4oz	225g	8oz
Vegetables, mixed, frozen, packet	1 x 500g		2 x 500g	
Cheese sauce	600ml	20fl oz	1l	32fl oz
Potatoes, cooked, sliced	500g	1lb	1kg	2lb
Cheese, grated	200g	7oz	400g	14oz

In a non-stick frying pan fry the onions in the oil until soft. In a saucepan, blanch (half cook) the frozen vegetables. Make a cheese sauce (see page 182) using half the grated cheese. Drain the vegetables. Mix together with the onions and place in an even layer in the Remoska. Season. Pour over the cheese sauce. Cover with overlapping slices of potato and sprinkle with the remaining cheese. Cook approx 30–40 minutes until the cheese melts and the top is light brown.

Timing is the same for the Standard and Grand.

Milena's Tip

The Remoska will cook any vegetable. Don't be afraid to experiment and try butternut squash, sweet potatoes or similar 'unusual' vegetables.

VEGETABLES IN FILO PASTRY

	Standard or Grand	
Serves	6	
Mushrooms	100g	4oz
Courgette	1	
Aubergine	1 small	
Peppers, red, green	1 each	
Onions	125g	5oz
Oil, olive	2 tbsp	
Tomato purée	1 tbsp	
Garlic purée	1 tsp	
Tomatoes	2	
Salt and black pepper		
Butter	100g	4oz
Filo pastry, packet	1 x 300g	

Cut all the vegetables into 1cm (½in) pieces. In a non-stick frying pan lightly fry the onions in the oil. Add the remaining ingredients except the butter and pastry and season to taste. Cook for approx 8–10 minutes, until soft and cool. Melt the butter. Lay out 6 single sheets of Filo pastry, lightly brush with the butter and cover with another sheet. Cut each double sheet of Filo into 6 squares. Spoon a good heaped tablespoon of the mixture into the centre of each square. Lightly brush the edge with the melted butter. Gather the edges up into the centre to form a parcel. Cook in the Remoska for approx 25 minutes until the pastry is crisp.

Timing is the same for the Standard and Grand.

VEGETABLE GRATIN

	Standard		Grand	
Serves	*4*		*6–8*	
Oil, olive	2 tbsp		3 tbsp	
Onions, red, sliced	2		4	
Peppers, yellow, sliced	2		4	
Courgettes, thick sliced	2 medium		4 medium	
Garlic clove, crushed	1		2	
Tomatoes, ripe, quartered	250g	9oz	500g	1lb
Mushrooms, chestnut, sliced	250g	9oz	500g	1lb
Passata	75ml	3fl oz	175ml	6fl oz
Salt and black pepper				
Egg	1 large		2 large	
Yogurt, Greek, low fat	2 tbsp		4 tbsp	
Cheese, Parmesan, grated	3 tbsp		6 tbsp	
Nutmeg, fresh, grated				

Heat half the oil in a large non-stick frying pan and cook the onions, peppers and courgettes over a high heat, stirring constantly, until tender and turning golden. Add the garlic with the rest of the oil and stir-fry for a few more minutes. Add the tomatoes, mushrooms, passata and seasoning and stir-fry for a few minutes more over a medium heat. Transfer the mixture into the Remoska and smooth the top.

Beat together the egg, yogurt, half the cheese, nutmeg and seasoning to taste, and pour the mixture over the vegetables. Sprinkle the rest of the cheese over the top. Cook for approx 30–35 minutes until golden and bubbling. Serve immediately.

If using the Grand cook for a further 10 minutes.

VEGETABLE CRUMBLE

	Standard		Grand	
Serves	*4*		*8–10*	
Cumin, ground	2 tsp		3 tsp	
Coriander, ground	2 tsp		3 tsp	
Turmeric	1 tsp		2 tsp	
Chilli powder	1/2 tsp		1 tsp	
Ginger, root, grated	1 tsp		2 tsp	
Oil	2 tbsp		3 tbsp	
Onion, chopped	1 large		2 large	
Garlic clove, crushed	1		2	
Peas, frozen	100g	4oz	200g	7oz
Celery, chopped	225g	8oz	350g	12oz
Carrots, diced	225g	8oz	350g	12oz
Tomato purée	1 tbsp		3 tbsp	
Stock, vegetable, hot	400ml	14fl oz	1l	32fl oz
Salt and black pepper				
Crumble				
Flour, wholewheat	75g	3oz	175g	6oz
Butter	50g	2oz	100g	4oz
Porridge oats	75g	3oz	175g	6oz
Oil	2 tbsp		4 tbsp	
Salt and black pepper				

Mix the spices and ginger to a paste with 2 or 3 tablespoons of cold water. In a large frying pan add the oil, fry the onion and garlic until soft, add the spice paste and cook for 5 minutes, stirring frequently. Add the vegetables, cook for another 5 minutes, add the tomato purée, stock and season. Transfer to the Remoska and cook for approx 20–25 minutes.

Crumble
Rub the flour and butter together, stir in the porridge oats and mix in the oil. Season to taste. Sprinkle the crumble on top of the vegetables and cook for approx 20–25 minutes until golden.

Timing is the same for the Standard and Grand.

POT

ATOES

Potatoes are an excellent source of fibre, minerals and vitamins – best when cooked in their skins.

POTATOES BAKED WITH VARIOUS FILLINGS

	Standard		Grand	
Serves	*4*		*8*	
Potatoes, large, washed	4		8	
Oil as needed				
Cheese filling				
Egg yolks	2		4	
Butter	50g	2oz	100g	4oz
Milk	50ml	2fl oz	100ml	4fl oz
Cheese, Cheddar, grated	2 tbsp		4 tbsp	
Parsley, fresh, chopped	2 tbsp		4 tbsp	
Salt and cayenne pepper				
Egg and Mushroom filling				
Onion, very finely chopped	1		2	
Garlic clove, crushed	1		2	
Mushrooms, finely chopped	100g	4oz	225g	8oz
Butter	25g	1oz	50g	2oz
Eggs, hard-boiled, finely chopped	2		4	
Milk	3–4 tbsp		6–8 tbsp	
Lemon, juice	1 tbsp		2 tbsp	
Salt and black pepper				

Wash and lightly oil the potatoes, place in the Remoska and cook for 1–1½hrs depending on the size.

Cheese filling
Mix together the egg yolks, butter, milk, cheese and parsley and season to taste with salt and cayenne pepper. When the potatoes are cooked, slice them in half lengthwise. Scoop out the flesh leaving the jacket ½cm (¼in) thick and mash the potato flesh into the mixture. Return the filled jackets to the Remoska and cook for a further 15–20 minutes.

Egg and Mushroom filling
Lightly fry the chopped onion, garlic and the mushrooms in the butter for about 5 minutes. Remove from the heat and mix in the eggs, a little milk, the lemon juice and season. When the potatoes are cooked, slice them in half lengthwise. Scoop out the flesh leaving the jacket ½cm (¼in) thick and mash the potato flesh into the filling. Place in the potato jackets, if you wish sprinkle with a little grated cheese. Return the filled jackets to the Remoska and cook for a further 15–20 minutes.

Timing is the same for the Standard and Grand.

Baked Potato

POTATO CAKES

	Standard		
Serves	*6*		
Potatoes, boiled and sieved	500g	1lb	
Butter	25g	1oz	
Cheese, Cheshire, grated	50g	2oz	
Egg, beaten	1 large		
Salt and black pepper			
Oil for greasing			

Use the Shallow Pan.

Mix together the potatoes, butter, cheese, half the egg and season, reserving the remainder of the egg. Form the mix into small cakes about 1cm (½in) thick. Lightly grease the Remoska and add the cakes. Add a little water to the remaining egg and brush the top of each cake. Cook for approx 15–20 minutes to light brown.

POTATOES BAKED WITH FENNEL, ONIONS & GARLIC

	Standard		Grand	
Serves	*4*		*6–8*	
Potatoes, waxy, wedges	500g	1lb	1kg	2lb
Garlic, cloves	10		15	
Shallots, whole, peeled	10		15	
Fennel bulbs, wedges	2		4	
Bay leaf	2		4	
Thyme, fresh, sprigs	6		8	
Rosemary, fresh, sprigs	2		4	
Stock, vegetable	100ml	4fl oz	400ml	14fl oz
Vinegar, sherry	2 tbsp		4 tbsp	
Sugar, caster	1 tsp		1 tbsp	
Fennel seeds	1 tsp		1 tbsp	
Paprika, sweet	1 tsp		3 tsp	
Oil, olive	3 tbsp		5 tbsp	
Salt and black pepper				

In a saucepan, boil the potatoes in salted water for 10–12 minutes, drain. Peel and finely chop 2 garlic cloves. Place the potatoes, shallots, the rest of the unpeeled cloves of garlic, fennel, bay leaf, thyme and rosemary sprigs in the Remoska. Mix together the stock, vinegar and sugar and pour over the vegetables. Stir in the fennel seeds, paprika, chopped garlic and oil, season with salt and freshly ground black pepper. Cook for approx 45 minutes–1 hour, until the vegetables are tender.

Timing is the same for the Standard and Grand.

Milena's Tip

In the UK, maincrop potatoes are available September to May. Look out for varieties Maris Piper, Pentland Crown, King Edward, and Desireé.

POTATOES BOMBAY

	Standard		Grand	
Serves	*4*		*6–8*	
Oil, vegetable	5 tbsp		7 tbsp	
Mustard seeds	1 tsp		2 tsp	
Onion, finely chopped	1 medium		2 medium	
Garlic purée	1 tsp		2 tsp	
Korma curry paste	1 tbsp		2 tbsp	
Potatoes, boiled and cubed	500g	1lb	700g	1¹/₂lb
Water, hot	4 tbsp		8 tbsp	
Salt to taste				

Heat the oil in the Remoska for 10–15 minutes, add the mustard seeds, onion, garlic purée and curry paste, stir lightly and cook for 15–20 minutes. Add the potatoes, hot water and salt, stir and cook for approx 20–25 minutes until the potatoes are hot.

Timing is the same for the Standard and Grand.

POTATO & CELERIAC BAKE

	Standard		Grand	
Serves	*4*		*8*	
Potatoes, small and thinly sliced	500g	1lb	1.5kg	3lb
Celeriac, peeled, thinly sliced	250g	9oz	500g	1lb
Onions, thinly sliced	100g	4oz	200g	7oz
Thyme, leaves, fresh	4 tsp		6 tsp	
Garlic cloves, chopped	2		4	
Salt and black pepper				
Stock, vegetable	250ml	8fl oz	450ml	15fl oz
Milk, skimmed	4 tbsp		8 tbsp	
Cheese, Parmesan, grated	4 tbsp		8 tbsp	
Butter	50g	2oz	100g	4oz

Layer the sliced potatoes, celeriac, onions, thyme leaves and garlic in the Remoska, seasoning each layer, starting and finishing with the potatoes. Pour over the stock and milk. Scatter the top with the Parmesan and little knobs of butter. Cook for approx 45–50 minutes until the vegetables are tender and the top is golden brown.

Timing is the same for the Standard and Grand.

POTATOES WITH CHEESE & CARAWAY

	Standard		Grand	
Serves	*4*		*8*	
Potatoes, scrubbed, thinly sliced	1kg	2lb	2kg	4lb
Onions, peeled, sliced	100g	4oz	225g	8oz
Garlic, cloves, crushed	2		4	
Milk as required				
Caraway seeds	1 tsp		3 tsp	
Parsley, fresh, chopped	1 tsp		3 tsp	
Salt and black pepper				
Cheese, grated	4 tbsp		8 tbsp	

Place the potatoes, onions, garlic, milk just to cover and caraway seeds into a saucepan and bring to the boil. Simmer gently for 5 minutes. Stir in the parsley and season to taste. Transfer the mixture to the Remoska and cover with the cheese. Cook for approx 35–40 minutes or until the potatoes are cooked and the cheese is golden brown and bubbling.

Timing is the same for the Standard and Grand.

POTATO & FRANKFURTER GOULASH

	Standard		Grand	
Serves	*4*		*6–8*	
Oil, olive	1 tbsp		2 tbsp	
Onion, finely chopped	1 large		2 large	
Garlic cloves, crushed	2		3	
Paprika, sweet	4 tsp		5–6 tsp	
Caraway seeds	2 tsp		3–4 tsp	
Potatoes, peeled and diced	500g	1lb	700g	1¹/₂lb
Salt and black pepper				
Stock, chicken	200ml	7fl oz	300ml	10fl oz
Frankfurter sausage, cut into 2cm (1¹/₂in) pieces	200g	7oz	400g	14oz
Marjoram, dried	1 tsp		2 tsp	
Crème fraîche	2 tbsp		4 tbsp	

Put the oil and onions into the Remoska and cook until golden. Add the garlic, paprika, caraway seeds, potatoes, salt and stock. Stir well to coat the potatoes with the other ingredients. Cook for approx 40 minutes or until the potatoes are cooked. Add the sausage pieces, season with black pepper, add the marjoram and cook for a further 15 minutes. Stir in the crème fraîche and serve hot.

Timing is the same for the Standard and Grand.

POTATO FANS

	Standard		Grand	
Serves	*6–8*		*8–10*	
Potatoes, peeled	6 medium		8 medium	
Butter	50g	2oz	100g	4oz
Milk	250ml	8fl oz	600ml	20fl oz
Salt and black pepper				

Cut a thin slice from the base of the potato to stand it upright. With a sharp knife make several cuts downwards to within 1cm ($\frac{1}{2}$in) of the base. Place in the Remoska, melt the butter and generously brush each potato. Pour the milk over the potatoes. Season and cook for approx 30–40 minutes to crisp and golden. Pinch the sides of the potatoes to open out the slices.

Timing is the same for the Standard and Grand.

POTATO GRATIN WITH HERBS

	Standard		Grand	
Serves	*4*		*8*	
Butter	25g	1oz	75g	3oz
Onions, sliced	50g	2oz	200g	7oz
Garlic clove, crushed	1		2	
Eggs	2		4	
Crème fraîche	150ml	5fl oz	300ml	10fl oz
Cream, double	150ml	5fl oz	300ml	10fl oz
Cheese, Gruyère, grated	100g	4oz	175g	6oz
Herbs, fresh, chopped, chervil, thyme, chives and parsley	4 tbsp		6 tbsp	
Potatoes, waxy, thinly sliced	700g	1¹/₂lb	1.5kg	3lb
Salt and black pepper				
Nutmeg, freshly grated	¹/₄ tsp		¹/₂ tsp	

Melt the butter in the Remoska and cook the onions and garlic until soft. In a large bowl, whisk together the eggs, crème fraîche, cream and half the cheese. Stir in the onion mixture, herbs, potatoes, salt, pepper and nutmeg. Pour into the Remoska and sprinkle the remaining cheese over the top. Cook for approx 50–60 minutes until golden brown.

Timing is the same for the Standard and Grand.

POTATO & GREEN BEAN CURRY

	Standard		Grand	
Serves	*4*		*6–8*	
Oil, vegetable	1 tbsp		2 tbsp	
Onion, finely sliced	1 large		2 large	
Ginger, fresh, grated	1 tsp		2 tsp	
Curry paste	2 tbsp		3–4 tbsp	
Water, hot	300ml	10fl oz	600ml	20fl oz
Green beans, sliced	200g	7oz	400g	14oz
Potatoes, peeled and diced	400g	14oz	700g	1¹/₂lb
Tomatoes, sliced	3		4	
Salt and black pepper				

Put the oil, onion and ginger into the Remoska and cook for 20 minutes. Stir in the curry paste and hot water. Add the beans, potatoes and tomatoes and season to taste. Cook for approx 45 minutes, or until the potatoes are cooked. Stir once during cooking.

Timing is the same for the Standard and Grand.

POTATOES WITH MIXED HERBS

	Standard	Grand
Serves	*4*	*6–8*
Potatoes, baking	4 medium	6 medium
Salt and black pepper		
Oil, olive	1 tbsp	2 tbsp
Herbs, mixed, dried	1 tsp	2 tsp

Cut each potato in half and score the cut surface diagonally, creating a diamond pattern. Season to taste and place in the Remoska cut side up. Drizzle with oil and sprinkle with herbs. Cook for approx 50–60 minutes until golden brown and cooked.

Timing is the same for the Standard and Grand.

POTATOES ROASTED WITH HERBS

	Standard		Grand	
Serves	*4*		*6–8*	
Oil, olive	2 tbsp		3 tbsp	
Rosemary, dried	3/4 tsp		1 tsp	
Mustard powder	3/4 tsp		1 tsp	
Sage, dried	1/2 tsp		1 tsp	
Thyme, dried	1/2 tsp		1 tsp	
Salt and black pepper				
Potatoes, small	700g	1 1/2 lb	1kg	2lb

In a large bowl, combine the oil, rosemary, mustard, sage, thyme and seasoning. Add the potatoes and toss to combine. If necessary cut larger potatoes into quarters or one inch pieces. Place in the Remoska and cook for approx 35–45 minutes until the potatoes are cooked.

Timing is the same for the Standard and Grand.

Milena's Tip

Always store potatoes in a dark, dry and cool place or they will go green. They are best kept away from any light.

POTATOES WITH RED PEPPER

	Standard		Grand	
Serves	*4*		*6–8*	
Potato, spicy wedges, frozen	500g	1lb	700g	1¹/₂lb
Pepper, red, deseeded and sliced	1		2	
Tomatoes, cherry	200g	7oz	300g	10oz
Oil, olive	1 tbsp		2 tbsp	
Garlic clove, crushed	2		3	
Spring onions, trimmed and sliced diagonally	6		8	
Salt and black pepper				

Put the potato wedges and red pepper into the Remoska and cook for 10 minutes. Add the tomatoes, oil, garlic and spring onions. Cook for approx 25 minutes until the potatoes are soft. Season to taste.

Timing is the same for the Standard and Grand.

Potatoes with Red Pepper

POTATOES WITH SAGE & AIOLI

	Standard		Grand	
Serves	*4–6*		*8*	
Oil, olive, for greasing				
Potatoes, finely sliced	1kg	2lb	1.8kg	4lb
Sage, dried	3 level tsp		6 level tsp	
Aioli (garlic sauce)	3 tbsp		6 tbsp	
Salt and black pepper				

Lightly grease the Remoska with the oil. Layer a third of the potatoes in the Remoska, sprinkle with a third of the sage and a third of aioli and season to taste. Repeat twice more. Cook for approx 50–60 minutes, or until the potatoes are cooked.

Timing is the same for the Standard and Grand.

Note Aioli is available from supermarkets and delicatessens.

Potatoes Roasted with Herbs and Garlic

POTATOES ROASTED WITH HERBS & GARLIC

	Standard		Grand	
Serves	*4*		*6–8*	
Potatoes, frozen, roasted	500g	1lb	700g	1^1/$_2$lb
Garlic cloves, cut in half	4		6	
Rosemary or thyme, fresh, few sprigs				
Oil, olive	1 tbsp		2 tbsp	
Salt and black pepper				

Place the potatoes, garlic and rosemary or thyme into the Remoska. Drizzle with the oil, season and cook for approx 25 minutes or until the potatoes are cooked.

Timing is the same for the Standard and Grand.

Potato Tortilla

POTATO TORTILLA

	Standard		Grand	
Serves	4		6–8	
Oil, olive	1 tbsp		2 tbsp	
Onion, finely sliced	1 large		2 large	
Potatoes, peeled and finely sliced	500g	1lb	700g	1¹/₂lb
Stock, vegetable, hot	150ml	5fl oz	300ml	10fl oz
Salt and black pepper				
Eggs	5		7	
Salt				
Oil, olive, for greasing				

Put the oil into the Remoska, add the onions. Layer the potatoes evenly over the onions. Add the stock, season and cook for approx 45 minutes or until the potatoes are cooked. Switch off. In a large bowl whisk the eggs until well blended, and add salt to taste. Carefully tip in the cooked potatoes and onions and gently stir to coat with the egg. Wipe the Remoska pan clean. Grease the Remoska with oil and pour in the potato and egg mixture. Cook until the tortilla is firm, approx 20–25 minutes. Serve hot, warm or cold, cut into slices or cubes and serve as a canapé.

Timing is the same for the Standard and Grand.

PO
&

ULTRY
GAME

When cooking poultry or game in the Remoska it is better to have the meat portioned as it takes less time to cook.

CHICKEN, BACON & MUSHROOM PARCELS

	Standard		Grand	
Serves	*4*		*8*	
Chicken breasts, skinless	4		8	
Lemon, juice	1/2		1	
Wine, white, dry	75ml	3fl oz	250ml	8fl oz
Parsley, fresh, flat-leaf, chopped	1 tbsp		3 tbsp	
Thyme, dried	1 tsp		2 tsp	
Salt and black pepper				
Mushrooms, small, chestnut	200g	7oz	400g	14oz
Garlic clove	1		2	
Margarine	1 tbsp		2 tbsp	
Bacon, rashers	4		8	
Oil	1 tsp		1 tbsp	
Parsley, fresh, to garnish				

Place the chicken breasts in a flat dish. In a bowl mix together the lemon juice, wine, herbs and seasoning. Stir in the sliced mushrooms. Spread the mixture over the chicken pieces, cover with cling film and marinate for 2 hours or overnight in the fridge. Mash the garlic into the margarine with a little seasoning.

Place each chicken breast with the mushroom topping in the centre of a piece of foil large enough to wrap the chicken loosely. Bring the foil up around the chicken to make a loose bowl shape. Divide the garlic paste between the parcels, putting a knob on top of each chicken portion, then seal securely, leaving an 'air gap'. Cook the parcels in the Remoska for approx 35–40 minutes, until the chicken is tender.

Meanwhile, cut the bacon rashers into strips, heat the oil in a non-stick pan and fry until crisp. To serve, remove each chicken portion and juices from the foil parcels, place on a plate and sprinkle with bacon. Garnish with the extra parsley.

Timing is the same for the Standard and Grand.

Milena's Tip

Chasseur is a sauce that is made with white wine, mushrooms, shallots, tomatoes and tarragon.

CHICKEN BREAST STUFFED WITH SEAFOOD

	Standard		Grand	
Serves	4		8	
Chicken breasts, skinless	4		8	
Filling				
Prawns, fresh, chopped	50g	2oz	100g	4oz
Salmon, fresh, chopped	50g	2oz	75g	3oz
Crab meat	50g	2oz	75g	3oz
Salt and black pepper				
Cream, double	1 tbsp		3 tbsp	
Wine, white, dry	175ml	6fl oz	300ml	10fl oz
Stock, chicken	300ml	10fl oz	450ml	15fl oz
Lemon butter sauce				
Butter, unsalted	225g	8oz	500g	1lb
Lemon, juice	1		1	
Egg, yolks	2		3	
Water, cold	50ml	2fl oz	100ml	4fl oz
Salt and black pepper				

Remove the little fillet from the bottom of the chicken breast and cut a slit to form a pocket along each breast.

Filling
Roughly mix together the prawns, salmon and crab meat. Season and bind with the cream. Divide into equal parts and stuff each breast. To hold the filling in place insert the little fillet after the stuffing. Arrange in the Remoska, season, and cover with the white wine and stock. Cook for approx 40–50 minutes, until the chicken is tender.

Lemon butter sauce
Melt the butter in a small saucepan. In a bowl whisk together the lemon juice, egg yolks and water. Place the bowl over a pan of boiling water and whisk continuously until the mixture thickens and leaves whisk marks. Remove from the heat and cool slightly. Gradually whisk in the warm butter until thoroughly combined. Season to taste, coat the chicken with the sauce just before serving.

Note
Take care not to add the butter too quickly or have the mixture too hot as the sauce will curdle.

Timing is the same for both the Standard and Grand.

CHICKEN WITH CASHEWS & WALNUTS, WRAPPED IN BACON

	Standard		Grand	
Serves	4		8	
Cashew nuts	40g	1¹/₂oz	75g	3oz
Walnuts	40g	1¹/₂oz	75g	3oz
Butter	75g	3oz	175g	6oz
Garlic purée	1 tsp		2 tsp	
Coriander seeds, crushed	1 tsp		2 tsp	
Breadcrumbs, fresh	75g	3oz	175g	6oz
Lemon, zest	1		1	
Lemon, juice	2 tbsp		3 tbsp	
Cream, double	1 tbsp		3 tbsp	
Bacon, streaky rashers	8		16	
Chicken breasts, skinless	4		8	

Toast the cashews and walnuts under the grill, lightly chop. Melt the butter, add the garlic and coriander. Mix together the nuts, breadcrumbs, lemon zest and juice, cream and half the melted butter mixture.

Beat out thinly the streaky bacon. Cut a deep slit in the side of each chicken breast to form a pocket. Stuff each pocket with the mixture. Wrap each breast in two slices of the bacon and brush with the remaining butter mix. Place in the Remoska and cook for approx 30–40 minutes, turning the breasts half way, until the chicken is tender.

Timing is the same for both the Standard and Grand.

CHICKEN CASSEROLE WITH COOK-IN SAUCE

	Standard		Grand	
Serves	4		8	
Chicken breasts, skinless	4		8	
Bacon, streaky rashers, diced	3		6	
Mushrooms, sliced	100g	4oz	200g	7oz
Leek, sliced	1		2	
Honey & Mustard Cook-In Sauce, jar	250g*		1 x 500g	

Fry the chicken in a non-stick frying pan until golden. Add the bacon, mushrooms and leeks and fry for a further 5 minutes. Transfer to the Remoska and pour over the sauce (*only use half a jar when using the Standard Remoska). Cook for approx 30 minutes until the chicken is cooked.

Timing is the same for the Standard and Grand.

CHICKEN WITH LEMON ON A BED OF ROAST VEGETABLES

	Standard		Grand	
Serves	*4*		*8*	
Chicken breasts, skinless	4		8	
Garlic, clove	1		2	
Sea salt				
Lemon, zest and juice	1/2		1	
Ginger, root, grated	1cm	1/2in	2cm	1in
Oil, groundnut	1 tbsp		2 tbsp	
Roast vegetables				
Potatoes, quartered	500g	1lb	1kg	2lb
Onion, chopped	1		2	
Carrot, sliced	1		2	
Sweet potato, peeled, sliced	1		2	
Leek, sliced	1/2		1	
Oil	1 tbsp		2 tbsp	
Salt and black pepper				

Place chicken pieces in a flat dish. Mash together the garlic and salt to a paste. Mix this with the lemon zest and juice, ginger and oil and coat the chicken pieces. Cover and leave to marinate for at least 30 minutes.

Roast vegetables
Place the roasting vegetables in the Remoska, sprinkle with oil and season to taste. Cook for 30 minutes. Place the chicken pieces on top of the vegetables, and pour the marinade over. Cook for approx 35–45 minutes until the chicken is tender.

Timing is the same for the Standard and Grand.

Milena's Tip

To check whether chicken is cooked, insert a skewer into the flesh – the juices should run clear.

CHICKEN LIVERS

	Standard		Grand	
Serves	*2*		*6*	
Oil, vegetable	1 tbsp		3 tbsp	
Onion, finely chopped	1 large		3 large	
Chicken livers	300g	10oz	700g	1¹/₂lb
Milk as needed				
Flour, plain, seasoned	3 tbsp		6 tbsp	
Salt and black pepper				

Heat the oil in the Remoska and add the onion. Cook until pale gold. Soak the chicken livers in enough milk to cover for 30 minutes – this takes out the bitter taste. Put the flour in a plastic bag. Drain the livers and dry with a paper towel. Place the livers in the plastic bag and shake well to coat. Add to the onion, stir well and cook for approx 15–20 minutes more, stirring once or twice. The livers will have a crispy crust and a soft centre.

Timing is the same for the Standard and Grand.

CHICKEN WITH MUSHROOMS & PASSATA

	Standard		Grand	
Serves	*4*		*8*	
Oil	1 tbsp		3 tbsp	
Chicken breasts, skinless	4		8	
Onion, chopped	1		2	
Garlic clove, crushed	1		2	
Salt and black pepper				
Passata, jar	1 x 350g		1 x 560g	
Thyme, leaves, fresh	2 tbsp		3 tbsp	
Pepper, green, sliced	1		2	
Pepper, yellow, sliced	1		2	
Mushrooms, sliced	100g	4oz	225g	8oz

Heat the oil in a non-stick frying pan and fry the chicken until golden. Transfer to the Remoska and add the onion, garlic and seasoning. Pour over the passata, add most of the thyme and stir well. Cook for 30 minutes. Stir in the peppers and mushrooms and cook for approx 40 minutes more until the chicken is tender. Sprinkle over the remaining thyme and serve.

Timing is the same for the Standard and Grand.

Chicken with Noodles and Coconut

CHICKEN WITH NOODLES & COCONUT

	Standard		Grand	
Serves	*4*		*6–8*	
Oil, vegetable	2 tbsp		4 tbsp	
Onion, finely sliced	1 large		2 large	
Garlic cloves, crushed	2		3–4	
Ginger, root, grated	2 tbsp		3–4 tbsp	
Spring onions, sliced diagonally	6		8	
Chicken breasts, skinless	500g	1lb	700g	1¹/₂lb
Jalfrezi curry paste	2 tbsp		4 tbsp	
Coconut milk, tin	1 x 400ml		2 x 400ml	
Stock, chicken, hot	300ml	10fl oz	450ml	15fl oz
Salt and black pepper				
Noodles, stir fry, ready to cook	200g	7oz	400g	14oz
Lime juice, fresh	2 tsp		2–4 tsp	
Sugar, soft brown	1 tsp		2 tsp	

Put the oil, onion, garlic, ginger and spring onions into the Remoska and cook until the onions are soft and golden. Add the chicken – cut into bite-sized pieces, curry paste, coconut milk, stock and season to taste. Stir to combine and cook for approx 20–30 minutes or until the chicken pieces are tender. Add the noodles to the Remoska and stir to coat with the sauce. Cook for approx 10 minutes or until the noodles are heated through. Add the lime juice and sugar, taste and adjust the seasoning if necessary.

Timing is the same for the Standard and Grand.

CHICKEN, POTATOES & VEGETABLES

	Standard		Grand	
Serves	*2*		*4*	
Stock, chicken, hot	150ml	5fl oz	300ml	10fl oz
Carrots, peeled and diced	3 medium		2 large	
Onions, finely diced	2 medium		1 large	
Mushrooms, button, sliced	100g	4oz	175g	6oz
Parsley, fresh, chopped	2 tbsp		4 tbsp	
Salt and black pepper				
Chicken legs	2		4	
Potatoes, peeled and diced	2 medium		4 medium	
Oil, olive, as needed				
Arrowroot	2 tsp		3 tsp	
Water, cold	2 tbsp		3 tbsp	
Cream, double	150ml	5fl oz	300ml	10fl oz

Pour the stock into the Remoska. Add the carrots, onions, mushrooms and parsley, and season to taste. Place the chicken legs on top of the vegetables, skin side down, and surround with the potato. Brush the chicken pieces with a little olive oil and season. Cook for 30 minutes. Turn the chicken pieces over and continue cooking for approx 30 minutes more or until the chicken is tender and the potatoes are soft. Remove the chicken and vegetables to a warm serving dish. Mix the arrowroot and water together and stir into the remaining liquid and cook for approx 5–10 minutes until thickened. Add the cream, mix together, and pour over the chicken and vegetables.

Timing is the same for the Standard and Grand.

Milena's Tip

Do not forget, as with all recipes, timing varies depending on the thickness of your meat and how finely you have chopped your ingredients.

CHICKEN WITH PEACHES

	Standard		Grand	
Serves	*4*		*6–8*	
Oil, vegetable	2 tbsp		4 tbsp	
Onion, finely sliced	1 medium		2 medium	
Pepper, green, sliced	1		2	
Peaches, sliced, tin	1 x 400g		2 x 400g	
Cornflour	1 tbsp		2 tbsp	
Soy sauce	1 tbsp		2 tbsp	
Cinnamon, ground	1 tsp		2 tsp	
Sugar	1 tsp		2 tsp	
Chicken breasts or thighs	500g	1lb	700g	1¹/₂lb

Put half the oil, the onion and the pepper into the Remoska and cook until soft. Whilst they are cooking, drain the tinned peaches and make up the liquid to 300ml (10fl oz) for the Standard, or 600ml (1pint) for the Grand with water, add the cornflour, soy sauce, cinnamon and sugar and mix together. Heat the remaining oil in a non-stick frying pan and brown the pieces of chicken. If using breasts cut each one into four; if using thighs, make two or three diagonal cuts in each. When the onions and peppers are soft, add the sauce, the peaches and the chicken. Cook for approx 30–40 minutes or until the chicken is tender, stir occasionally.

Timing is the same for the Standard and Grand.

Chicken with Peaches

CHICKEN & POTATO SAUTÉ

	Standard		Grand	
Serves	*4–6*		*8–10*	
Chicken breasts, skinless	500g	1lb	1kg	2lb
Paprika, sweet	3 tsp		4 tsp	
Potatoes, thickly sliced	350g	12oz	1kg	2lb
Oil, olive	2 tbsp		4 tbsp	
Garlic cloves, crushed	2		3	
Ginger, fresh, grated	4cm	2in	6cm	3in
Chilli pepper	1		2	
Spring onions, sliced	4		8	
Cumin, ground	2 tsp		3 tsp	
Tomatoes, chopped, tin	1 x 200g		1 x 400g	
Pepper, red, diced	1		2	
Wine, white	150ml	5fl oz	300ml	10fl oz
Salt and black pepper				
Parsley, fresh, chopped	4 tbsp		6 tbsp	
Coriander, fresh, chopped	4 tbsp		6 tbsp	

Cut the chicken breasts into strips, sprinkle with 2 teaspoons of paprika for the Standard, 3 teaspoons of paprika for the Grand, and leave to marinate for a few minutes. In a separate saucepan boil the potatoes for 6–7 minutes. Drain and leave to cool. Heat the oil in the Remoska, add the chicken and lightly brown. Remove the chicken and place on one side and keep warm. Add the garlic, ginger, chilli and spring onions, cook for 5 minutes. Stir in the cumin and the remainder of the paprika, continue to cook for 4–5 minutes. Add the drained tomatoes, potatoes, chicken, red pepper and wine. Season to taste and cook for approx 30–40 minutes until the chicken is tender. Stir in the parsley and coriander and serve.

Timing is the same for the Standard and Grand.

Milena's Tip

Do not marinate food in a metal dish as any acidic ingredients like vinegar or lemon juice can react with the metal and spoil the taste.

Chicken and Onion Curry

CHICKEN & ONION CURRY

	Standard		Grand	
Serves	*3–4*		*6–8*	
Oil, vegetable	3 tbsp		4 tbsp	
Onions, finely sliced	400g	14oz	500g	1lb
Ginger, fresh, grated	2 tsp		3 tsp	
Garlic cloves, crushed	2		3	
Garam masala paste	2–3 tsp		3–4 tsp	
Curry powder	2–3 tsp		3–4 tsp	
Tomato paste	2 tbsp		3 tbsp	
Chilli, red, fresh, deseeded and finely chopped (optional)	1–2		2	
Chicken thighs, skinned and scored diagonally	6		10	
Water, hot	300ml	10fl oz	400ml	14fl oz
Coriander, fresh, chopped	2 tbsp		4 tbsp	

Place the oil and onions into the Remoska and cook until the onions are soft and golden. Add the ginger, garlic, garam masala and curry powder and cook for 10 minutes. Stir in the tomato paste and chilli (if using) add the chicken pieces, turning to coat with the onion mixture. Pour in the water, add the coriander and cook for approx 50–60 minutes or until the chicken is tender.

Timing is the same for the Standard and Grand.

CHICKEN ON A RACK

	Standard	Grand
Serves	*4*	*8*
Chicken drumsticks	4	8
Chicken thighs	4	8
Garlic clove, crushed with salt	1	2
Mustard, grainy	2 tsp	1 tbsp
Oil, olive	1 tbsp	2 tbsp
Honey	2 tsp	1 tbsp

The Remoska rack is recommended for this recipe.

Place the chicken in a flat dish. Mix the rest of the ingredients together and spread over the chicken. Cover with cling film and refrigerate for 30 minutes. Place on the rack in the Remoska and cook for approx 30–40 minutes until the chicken is tender. If too much juice accumulates, pour some off half way through the cooking. This will help to crisp up the chicken.

Timing is the same for the Standard and Grand.

CHICKEN PROVENÇAL

	Standard		Grand	
Serves	*4*		*6–8*	
Butter	50g	2oz	100g	4oz
Garlic cloves, unpeeled	1		3	
Onion, sliced	1		2	
Aubergine, thickly sliced	1		2	
Courgette, thickly sliced	2		3	
Tomato purée	1 tbsp		2 tbsp	
Chicken, skinned, jointed	1.5kg	3lb	2.5kg	5lb
Herbs, fresh, mixed, chopped	1 tbsp		3 tbsp	
Sherry, wine	200ml	7fl oz	400ml	14fl oz
Tomatoes, chopped, tin	1 x 450g		2 x 450g	

Heat the butter in the Remoska, add the garlic cloves, onions, aubergine, courgette
and tomato purée. Cook for approx 20–30 minutes. Meanwhile, brown the chicken
pieces in a non-stick frying pan, transfer to the Remoska. Add half the herbs and the
sherry. Cook for approx 20–25 minutes, add the tomatoes and continue to cook for
approx 30–40 minutes more until the chicken pieces are tender. Remove the chicken
pieces, transfer the liquid and vegetable contents to a saucepan and reduce by half.
Replace the chicken in the Remoska, cover with the sauce and reheat. Sprinkle with
the remaining mixed herbs.

Timing is the same for the Standard and Grand.

DUCK LEGS WITH ONIONS

	Standard	Grand
Serves	*2*	*4–6*
Duck legs	2	4–6
Caraway seeds, crushed	2 tsp	4 tsp
Onions, quartered	2 large	4 large
White Wine Gravy Mix, packet	1	2

Rub the caraway seeds all over the duck legs, place in the Remoska and start cooking. After 20 minutes or so, when the fat begins to run pour it off and carry on cooking. If too much fat gathers after a further 15–20 minutes pour most of that off. At this point add the onions, stir so that the duck legs are sitting on the onions and leave to cook until the legs are really crisp, approx a further 20 minutes. Prepare the gravy mix using a little extra wine instead of water. When the duck is ready, pour two thirds of the gravy mix into the Remoska, stir and cook for approx 5–10 minutes for the gravy to cook and thicken. Cook the rest of the gravy separately in a small saucepan or microwave according to instruction on the packet.

Timing is the same for the Standard and Grand.

GUINEA FOWL POT ROAST

	Standard		Grand	
Serves	*2–3*		*4–6*	
Oil	1 tbsp		2 tbsp	
Leeks, sliced	2		3	
Carrots, sliced	3		4	
Bacon, smoked, small cubes	2 tbsp		3 tbsp	
Thyme, fresh, sprigs	3		4	
Salt and black pepper				
Lemon	1/2		1	
Garlic cloves, halved	2		4	
Guinea fowl	1		2	
Wine, white	250ml	8fl oz	400ml	14fl oz
Butter				

Heat the oil in a non-stick frying pan and lightly fry the leeks, carrots, and bacon, and transfer to the Remoska. Add the thyme and season. Place the lemon and the garlic inside the bird(s) and sit on the vegetables. Add the wine, butter the breast and legs of the birds and cook for approx 1 hour in the Standard, 1$\frac{1}{2}$ hours in the Grand, or until the meat is tender.

Coq au Vin

COQ AU VIN

	Standard		Grand	
Serves	*4*		*6–8*	
Bacon lardons	75g	3oz	225g	8oz
Mushrooms, sliced	175g	6oz	300g	10oz
Onions, sliced	4		6	
Butter	25g	1oz	50g	2oz
Oil	2 tbsp		3 tbsp	
Chicken pieces	500g	1lb	1kg	2lb
Wine, red	400ml	14fl oz	750ml	28fl oz
Cornflour	2 tsp		1 tbsp	
Brandy	1 tbsp		2 tbsp	
Sugar	1 tsp		2 tsp	
Nutmeg, fresh, grated	$1/4$ tsp		$1/4$ tsp	
Salt and black pepper				
Bouquet garni sachet	1		2	

In a large non-stick frying pan fry the bacon, mushrooms and onions in the butter and oil until golden brown. Place half the mixture in the Remoska. Fry the chicken pieces in the same frying pan until they are golden brown and place on top of the mixture in the Remoska. Add the remaining mixture.

Gradually stir the blended wine and cornflour into the pan used for frying, bring to the boil and simmer for 1–2 minutes. Add the brandy and pour over the chicken pieces. Add the sugar, nutmeg, salt and pepper, the bouquet garni and cook for approx 1 hour or until the chicken is tender.

Timing is the same for the Standard and Grand.

TURKEY GOULASH

	Standard		Grand	
Serves	*4*		*8*	
Oil	2 tbsp		3 tbsp	
Onion, chopped	1		2	
Flour, plain	50g	2oz	100g	4oz
Paprika, sweet	1 tsp		2 tsp	
Cayenne pepper	$^1/_4$ tsp		$^1/_2$ tsp	
Tomatoes, chopped, tin	1 x 400g		2 x 400g	
Stock, chicken	600ml	20fl oz	900ml	1$^1/_2$pt
Carrot, chopped	250g	9oz	500g	1lb
Potatoes, diced	250g	9oz	500g	1lb
Pepper, green, diced	1		2	
Tomato purée	100g	4oz	200g	7oz
Salt and black pepper				
Turkey, cooked, diced	500g	1lb	1kg	2lb
Yogurt, Greek, plain	250ml	8fl oz	450ml	15fl oz

In a non-stick frying pan fry the onion in the oil until softened. Stir in the flour, paprika, cayenne pepper and the tomatoes and transfer to the Remoska. Add the stock, the rest of the vegetables, tomato purée and seasoning. Stir and cook for approx 30–40 minutes. Add the turkey and allow to heat through for approx 10–15 minutes. Stir in the yogurt before serving.

Timing is the same for the Standard and Grand.

Milena's Tip

Remember, NEVER immerse the Remoska lid in water.
When in use, it is the lid that does the cooking, like opening an oven door, it will be hot. Handle with care.

GUINEA FOWL IN WINE & MUSHROOM SAUCE

	Standard		Grand	
Serves	*2–3*		*4–6*	
Flour, for coating				
Guinea fowl, jointed	1		2	
Oil	1 tbsp		2 tbsp	
Mushrooms, sliced	175g	6oz	350g	12oz
Wine, white	200ml	7fl oz	400ml	14fl oz
Stock, chicken	150ml	5fl oz	250ml	8fl oz
Cornflour	2 tsp		3 tsp	
Cream, single	4 tbsp		6 tbsp	
Salt and black pepper				

Lightly coat the guinea fowl joints with the flour. Heat the oil in a non-stick frying pan and brown the joints a few at a time. Place in the Remoska, add the mushrooms, wine and stock and cook for approx 40–50 minutes, until tender. Mix the cornflour with a little water and stir in the cream. Add to the Remoska and cook for a further 7–10 minutes to thicken the sauce.

Timing is the same for the Standard and Grand.

Guinea Fowl in Wine & Mushroom Sauce

TURKEY STEAKS WITH HAM, CHEESE & APPLE

	Standard	Grand
Serves	*4*	*6*
Oil, vegetable	1 tbsp	2 tbsp
Turkey steaks	4	6
Ham, boiled, slices	4	6
Apples, rings, 1/2cm (1/4in)	8	12
Cheese, slices	4	8

Use the Shallow Pan.

Heat the oil in a non-stick frying pan. Flatten the turkey steaks and fry on both sides. Place in the Remoska, cover each steak with ham, two apple rings and a slice of cheese. Cook until the cheese melts, approx 15–25 minutes, depending which cheese or size of Remoska you use.

TURKEY MEAT LOAF

	Standard		Grand	
Serves	*4*		*8*	
Tomato purée	175g	6oz	350g	12oz
Wine, red, dry	150ml	5fl oz	300ml	10fl oz
Water, cold	150ml	5fl oz	300ml	10fl oz
Garlic clove, finely chopped	1		2	
Basil, dried	1/2 tsp		1 tsp	
Oregano, dried	1/4 tsp		1/2 tsp	
Salt	1/4 tsp		1/2 tsp	
Turkey breast, minced	500g	1lb	1kg	2lb
Oats, rolled	100g	4oz	225g	8oz
Egg	1		2	
Courgette, grated	50g	2oz	100g	4oz

Combine the tomato purée, wine, water, garlic, basil, oregano and salt in a saucepan. Bring to the boil, reduce to low and simmer, uncovered for 15 minutes. Set aside.

Combine the turkey, oats, egg, courgette and a third of the tomato mixture in a large bowl. Mix well. Shape into a loaf and place in the Remoska. Cook for approx 45 minutes. Pour half of the remaining tomato mixture over the top of the loaf and cook for a further 15 minutes. Place on a serving dish and cool for 10 minutes before slicing. Serve hot or cold with the remaining tomato sauce.

If using the Grand make two loaves and cook side by side and adding a further 10 minutes to the cooking time.

Turkey Bean Bake

TURKEY BEAN BAKE

	Standard		Grand	
Serves	*4*		*6-8*	
Aubergine, sliced	3		4	
Oil, olive for brushing				
Onion, finely sliced	1 medium		2 medium	
Turkey breast, diced	500g	1lb	1kg	2lb
Salt and black pepper				
Beans, red kidney, tin	1 x 425g		2 x 425g	
Tomatoes, chopped, tin	1 x 400g		2 x 400g	
Thyme, fresh, chopped	2 tbsp		4 tbsp	
Chilli sauce	3 tsp		6 tsp	
Cheese, cheddar, grated	6 tbsp		12 tbsp	

Brush each slice of aubergine with oil and fry in a non-stick frying pan in batches until golden on both sides. Transfer each batch to a plate lined with kitchen roll. When they are all cooked add a little more olive oil to the frying pan and cook the onion until soft. Add the turkey, season well using more black pepper than salt and cook until brown. Stir in the rinsed and drained kidney beans, tomatoes, thyme and chilli sauce and bring to the boil and simmer to reduce the liquid. Cover the base of the Remoska with a third of the aubergine slices, then half of the turkey and bean mixture, repeat ending with a layer of aubergines. Sprinkle with the cheese and cook until the cheese is melted and golden brown.

STUFFED TURKEY STEAKS

	Standard		Grand	
Serves	*4*		*6*	
Stuffing				
Bread, thick slices, diced	3		6	
Milk	3 tbsp		6 tbsp	
Butter	25g	1oz	50g	2oz
Egg, yolk	1		2	
Lemon, zest, grated	1/2		1	
Nutmeg, fresh, grated	to taste		to taste	
Parsley, fresh, chopped	1 tbsp		2 tbsp	
Salt and black pepper				
Egg, white	1		2	
Almonds, ground	1 tbsp		2 tbsp	
Turkey steaks, thick	4		6	
Flour, plain	1 tbsp		2 tbsp	
Oil, vegetable	2 tbsp		3 tbsp	
Wine, white	100ml	4fl oz	200ml	7fl oz
Stock, chicken or vegetable	100m	4fl oz	200ml	7fl oz
Salt and black pepper				

Stuffing
Sprinkle the milk on the bread. Toss lightly to dampen but not to disintegrate. Cream the butter with the egg yolk, stir in the damp bread, lemon zest, nutmeg, and parsley. Season. Whisk the egg white until stiff and fold in together with the ground almonds.

Make a slit in each of the steaks to make a pocket, flatten them with a rolling pin or a meat mallet to make them bigger. Fill the pocket with the stuffing and fasten with a cocktail stick. Lightly flour each steak. Heat the oil in a non-stick frying pan and brown the meat on both sides. Transfer to the Remoska, add the wine and cook until the wine has evaporated, this is difficult to time exactly, approx 15–20 minutes. Add the stock and seasoning and cook until tender, approx 25–35 minutes more, turning the steaks once.

If using the Grand increase cooking time by a further 10–15 minutes until tender.

VENISON CASSEROLE

	Grand	
Serves	6	
Venison, medallions	1kg	2lb
Oil, olive	50ml	2fl oz
Onions, thinly sliced	700g	1¹/₂lb
Garlic cloves, crushed	4	
Sugar, light brown	2 tbsp	
Flour, plain	3 tbsp	
Pale ale or lager	600ml	20fl oz
Stock, beef	250ml	8fl oz
Bay leaf	1	
Thyme, fresh, sprigs	2 large	
Salt and black pepper		
Vinegar, white wine or cider	3 tbsp	
Parsley, fresh, to garnish		

Make a five layer 'foil cover' to fit inside the Remoska. This slows down the cooking. Cut each medallion horizontally into two chunky pieces. Heat the oil in a large heavy-based non-stick frying pan and brown the venison in batches over a high heat.

Transfer to the Remoska using a slotted spoon. Add the onions to the oil remaining in the frying pan and cook for 10 minutes, stirring until they begin to soften. Add the garlic and sugar, mix well and cook gently for 10 minutes or until they begin to brown and caramelise.

Stir in the flour, gradually add the beer, stirring. Bring to the boil, scraping up any sediment from the bottom of the pan, then pour over the venison in the Remoska. Pour the stock over the venison and onions and add the herbs and plenty of pepper. Stir lightly to mix. Cover with the foil and cook for approx 1 hour. Carefully stir in the vinegar and cook for a further 30 minutes or until the venison is very tender. Check the seasoning and garnish with chopped parsley.

VENISON SAUSAGE & BACON CASSEROLE

	Standard		Grand	
Serves	*4*		*6*	
Oil, vegetable	1 tbsp		2 tbsp	
Onion, finely chopped	1 large		2 large	
Sausages, venison, halved	6–8		10–12	
Bacon, smoked, thick slices, diced	4		6	
Flour, plain	25g	1oz	50g	2oz
Tomatoes, chopped, tin	1 x 400g		*see below	
Soy sauce	2 tsp		1 tbsp	
Oregano, dried	1/2 tsp		1 tsp	
Bay leaf	1		2	
Salt and black pepper				

Heat the oil in the Remoska. Cook the onion for 10 minutes, add the sausages and bacon and cook for approx 10 minutes stirring once or twice. Stir in the flour, tomatoes, (*use one and a half tins if using the Grand Remoska) soy sauce, oregano and bay leaf, season and cook for approx 30–40 minutes more.

.

Timing is the same for the Standard and Grand.

Milena's Tip

Although venison is red meat, it is lower in fat than chicken. Farmed venison is a good alternative for people watching their fat intake.

VENISON STEAK WITH CRANBERRY SAUCE

	Standard	Grand
Serves	*4*	*8*
Sauce		
Cranberry jelly	3 tbsp	5 tbsp
Lemon, zest and juice	1	2
Orange, zest and juice	1	2
Mustard, Dijon	2 tsp	1 tbsp
Port	4 tbsp	8 tbsp
Oil, olive	1 tbsp	2 tbsp
Shallots, chopped fine	2	4
Peppercorns, crushed	as required	as required
Venison steaks	4	8

Sauce
In a saucepan heat the cranberry jelly, the lemon and orange zest and juice and the mustard to simmering point. Remove from the heat and add the port.

In the Remoska heat the oil and fry the shallots until soft. Season the venison steaks with the crushed peppercorns, place in the Remoska and cook for approx 10 minutes in the Standard, 15–20 minutes in the Grand, depending how you like your steak. To serve cover with sauce.

Milena's Tip

Venison under three years old is best and meat always improves when it is marinated.

MEAT

Make friends with your

local butcher!

BARBECUE SPARE RIBS

	Standard		Grand	
Serves	*4*		*8*	
Pork ribs	**1kg**	**2lb**	**1¹/₂kg**	**3lb**
Barbecue Sauce				
Sherry	300ml	10fl oz	600ml	20fl oz
Soy sauce	175ml	6fl oz	350ml	12fl oz
Honey	175g	6oz	350g	12oz
Sugar, demerara	50g	2oz	100g	4oz
Tomato ketchup	75g	3oz	150g	5¹/₂oz
Tomato purée	50g	2oz	100g	4oz
Garlic purée	50g	2oz	100g	4oz
Ginger, grated	1 tbsp		2 tbsp	

In a saucepan bring the ribs to the boil in water, drain and rinse in cold water. In fresh water bring to the boil again and simmer for 30 minutes, then drain. Meanwhile, mix together all the ingredients for the sauce. Place the ribs in the Remoska and lightly cover with some of the sauce. The remaining sauce may be put into a jar and kept in the refrigerator for future use. Cook the ribs for approx 40–50 minutes until they are brown and sticky.

Timing is the same for the Standard and Grand.

SPICED BEEFBURGERS

	Standard		Grand	
Serves	*4*		*8*	
Bread, white	50g	2oz	100g	4oz
Milk	50ml	2fl oz	100ml	4fl oz
Oil	1 tbsp		2 tbsp	
Onion, finely chopped	75g	3oz	175g	6oz
Beef, lean, minced	500g	1lb	1kg	2lb
Herbs, mixed, dried	¹/₂ tsp		1 tsp	
Chilli flakes	¹/₄ tsp		¹/₂ tsp	
Worcester sauce	¹/₂ tsp		1 tsp	
Salt and black pepper				
Oil, for cooking	2 tbsp		3 tbsp	

Soak the bread in the milk. In a non-stick frying pan fry the onion in the oil until soft. Squeeze the milk from the bread and mix all the remaining ingredients together, except the oil for cooking. Divide into equal parts and shape into burgers. Heat the cooking oil in the Remoska and cook the burgers, approx 10–15 minutes each side depending how thick and rare you like them.

Timing is the same for the Standard and Grand.

BEEF CARBONADE

	Standard		Grand	
Serves	*4*		*6*	
Beef dripping	2 tbsp		3 tbsp	
Onions, sliced	2 large		3 large	
Garlic cloves	2		3	
Flour, plain	1 tbsp		3 tbsp	
Mustard powder	1 tsp		1 tsp	
Salt and black pepper				
Beef, shin, cubed	700g	1^1/$_2$lb	1.5kg	3lb
Beer	200 ml	7fl oz	300ml	10fl oz
Stock, beef	175ml	6fl oz	300ml	10fl oz
Sugar, dark brown	1 tsp		2 tsp	
Thyme, fresh, sprig	2		3	
Bay leaf	1		2	
Celery stick, diced	1		2	
Topping				
Butter	25g	1oz	50g	4oz
Garlic clove	1		2	
Mustard, Dijon	2 tsp		1 tbsp	
Parsley, fresh, chopped	2 tbsp		4 tbsp	
Baguette loaf, slices	8–10		12–14	

Heat half of the dripping in a large non-stick frying pan and cook the onions and garlic until softened. Transfer to the Remoska. In a bowl mix together the flour, mustard, seasoning and toss the meat in the flour. Add the remaining dripping to the frying pan and heat. Brown the meat and transfer to the Remoska. Add the beer, stock, sugar, thyme, bay leaf and celery. Season and cook until the casserole has started to boil. Take off the lid and cover the casserole with a piece of foil (this ensures the casserole doesn't cook too quickly). Cook for approx 1 hour more, checking it is not too dry – add a little more stock if necessary. Test for tenderness, allow an extra 30 minutes cooking time if necessary.

Topping
Cream the butter with the garlic, mustard and half of the parsley. Spread thickly over the slices of bread. Remove the 'foil lid' and arrange the bread slices to cover the top of the casserole. Cook for 15-20 minutes or until the bread is browned and crisp. Scatter the remaining chopped parsley over the top and serve.

Timing is the same for the Standard and Grand.

CASSOULET

Serves	Grand	
	8	
Pork, belly	350g	12oz
Oil, olive	3 tbsp	
Chicken legs and thighs	8	
Sausages, Toulouse or Italian coarse pork	500g	1lb
Onions, chopped	2 medium	
Carrot, chopped	1 large	
Garlic cloves, crushed	3–4	
Bay leaves	3	
Thyme, dried	2 tsp	
Tomato purée	3 tbsp	
Tomatoes, sun dried, chopped	12	
Beans, butter, tin	4 x 410g	
Salt and black pepper		
Butter	75g	3oz
Breadcrumbs, fresh, white	100g	4oz

Cube the belly pork, heat 2 tablespoons of the oil in a non-stick frying pan, brown the pork in batches and transfer to a plate. Heat the remaining oil and fry the chicken legs and thighs until golden. Transfer to the same plate. Brown the sausages the same way and add to the plate. Add the onions, the carrot, garlic, bay leaves, thyme, tomato purée and the tomatoes to the same pan. Cook for approx 5 minutes until the vegetables start to soften. Place half the beans and liquid in the Remoska, add a layer of all the meats, then the onion and tomato mixture, season well and cover with the remaining beans and liquid. Melt the butter in a clean non-stick frying pan and stir in the breadcrumbs. Spread the breadcrumbs evenly over the beans. Cook for approx 1 hour until a golden crust has formed. If browning too quickly, cover with foil.

Milena's Tip

When making Yorkshire pudding, try using semi-skimmed milk instead of half full fat milk and half water, you should get the same results.

Beef Wellington

BEEF WELLINGTON

	Standard		Grand	
Serves	2		4	
Beef fillet	175g	6oz	350g	12oz
Oil	1 tbsp		1–2 tbsp	
Onion, finely chopped	50g	2oz	100g	4oz
Mushrooms, finely chopped	50g	2oz	100g	4oz
Pastry, puff	225g	8oz	500g	1lb
Salt and black pepper				
Pâté	50g	2oz	100g	4oz
Egg, beaten	1		1	

Cut the fillet in two, or four rounds if using the Grand. Heat the oil in a non-stick frying pan, quickly seal on both sides and set aside. Fry the onions until soft, without colour, add the mushrooms and cook for a further 5 minutes. Cool.

Divide the puff pastry and roll into 12cm (5in) squares. Place a fillet in the centre and slightly season. Place the onion and mushroom mixture on the top of the fillets. Divide the pâté into required slices and place on top. Lightly brush the edges of the pastry with beaten egg and gather up into a parcel. Brush with the beaten egg and score the top once or twice. Cook in the Remoska for approx 35 minutes.

Timing is the same for the Standard and Grand.

STUFFED & ROLLED LAMB BREAST

	Standard			Grand		
Serves	*3–4*			*6–8*		
Lamb, boned breast	1			2		
Stuffing						
Breadcrumbs, fresh	100g	4oz		200g	7oz	
Parsley, fresh, chopped	1 tbsp			2 tbsp		
Apricots, dried, soaked, chopped	100g	4oz		200g	7oz	
Butter	50g	2oz		100g	4oz	
Walnuts, roughly chopped	50g	2oz		100g	4oz	
Egg	1 large			2 large		
Salt and black pepper						
Basic ingredients for gravy						
Stock, lamb	150ml	5fl oz		300ml	10fl oz	

Ask your butcher to bone a breast of lamb and trim off as much fat as possible including the top layer of the skin. Mix all the stuffing ingredients together. Spread the stuffing over the meat, roll it up and tie with string. Season.

Start cooking a basic gravy (see page 181). Cook for 20 minutes and transfer the mix to the Remoska. Place the meat on top and leave to cook for at least 20–30 minutes. Turn the meat and carry on cooking for a further 20–30 minutes. Turn again adding the stock. Cook for a further 30–40 minutes or until the meat is roasted to a golden brown. Remove from the Remoska, keep warm and continue to finish the gravy as indicated in the recipe for the basic gravy, serve in a sauceboat.

When using the Grand, cook for approx 10–15 minutes extra.

Milena's Tip

Use a potato peeler to pare thin slices of the zest from a lemon or orange.

LAMB CASSEROLE WITH SHALLOTS

	Standard		Grand	
Serves	*4*		*6*	
Lamb shoulder, boned, cubed	500g	1lb	1kg	2lb
Garlic clove	1		2	
Lemon, zest and juice	1		1¹/₂	
Oil, olive	4 tbsp		5 tbsp	
Flour, plain	3 tbsp		4 tbsp	
Salt and black pepper				
Shallots, peeled, whole	300g	10oz	400g	14oz
Anchovy fillets	4		5	
Sugar, caster	¹/₂ tsp		1 tsp	
Wine, white, fruity	200ml	7fl oz	400ml	14fl oz
Stock, lamb	200ml	7fl oz	600ml	20fl oz
Bay leaf	1		2	
Thyme, fresh, sprig	2		3	
Parsley, fresh, sprig	1		2	
Potatoes, small, new, not peeled	300g	10oz	500g	1lb
Cream, double	2 tbsp		4 tbsp	
Parsley, fresh, chopped	2 tbsp		4 tbsp	

Mix the lamb with the garlic, the lemon zest, half the juice of the lemon and half of the oil. Leave to marinate for 12–24 hours. Drain the lamb, pat dry, keep the marinade. Heat the rest of the oil in a non-stick frying pan. Place the flour in a plastic bag, season, add the lamb, shake to coat, removing any excess. Seal the lamb on all sides in the hot oil. Do this in batches, transferring each batch to the Remoska. You may need to add an extra 1–2 tablespoons of oil to the frying pan.

Reduce the heat under the frying pan, add more oil if necessary and cook the shallots gently over a very low heat until soft and golden but not browned. Add the anchovies and sugar and cook, mashing the anchovies into the onion with a wooden spoon. Add the reserved marinade, pour in the wine and stock and bring to the boil. Simmer for approx 5 minutes and pour over the lamb in the Remoska. Tie the bay leaf, thyme and parsley together, add to the lamb and season. Make a round 'foil lid' by layering 4–5 sheets of foil to fit inside the Remoska and place over the lamb. (This helps to slow down the cooking). Cook for approx 45 minutes, add the potatoes to the Remoska and stir, cook for approx 35 minutes to 1 hour until the lamb is tender (the time depends on the thickness of the meat). Drizzle in the cream and the rest of the lemon juice. Garnish with chopped parsley.

Timing is the same for the Standard and Grand.

COUNTRY LAMB CASSEROLE

	Standard		Grand	
Serves	4		8	
Lamb chops	500g	1lb	1kg	2lb
Oil	2 tbsp		4 tbsp	
Garlic clove, finely chopped	1		2	
Potatoes, medium size	500g	1lb	1kg	2lb
Onions	8 small		16 small	
Beans, French, may be frozen	175g	6oz	350g	12oz
Cloves, ground, to taste				
Mushroom soup, condensed, tin	1 x 320g		2 x 320g	
Stock, lamb	150ml	5fl oz	300ml	10fl oz
Salt and black pepper				
Paprika, sweet				

Trim excess fat from the chops. Heat the oil in a non-stick frying pan, add the garlic and fry the lamb on both sides. Place in the Remoska and arrange the halved potatoes and onions around the lamb. Add the beans, cloves, soup, stock and season to taste. Cook for approx 1hr 15 minutes in the Standard or 1hr 45 minutes in the Grand until the lamb is tender. Sprinkle with a little paprika before serving.

LAMB KEBABS

	Standard		Grand	
Serves	4		8–10	
Marinade				
Lime, juice	2		4	
Tomato purée	50g	2oz	100g	4oz
Garlic purée	25g	1oz	50g	2oz
Chilli, sweet	25g	1oz	25g	1oz
Oil, olive	50ml	2fl oz	100ml	4fl oz
Pork, lamb or chicken, cubed	500g	1lb	1kg	2lb
Pepper, red	1		2	
Pepper, green	1		2	
Onions	2		4	
Mushrooms	12 small		24 small	
Kebab sticks				
Salt and black pepper				

Squeeze juice from the limes, mix with the purées, chilli and oil. Put the meat into the marinade for 30 minutes. Cut the peppers and onions into chunks and thread alternately with the meat and mushrooms onto the sticks. Season, place into the Remoska and cook for approx 30 minutes.

Timing is the same for the Standard and Grand.

Greek Style Lamb Pie

GREEK STYLE LAMB PIE

	Standard		Grand	
Serves	*4*		*8*	
Lamb, minced	500g	1lb	1kg	2lb
Onion, sliced	1 medium		2 medium	
Garlic clove, crushed	1		2	
Tomatoes, tin	1 x 400g		2 x 400g	
Mint, fresh, chopped	2 tbsp		4 tbsp	
Nutmeg, fresh, grated	1 tsp		2 tsp	
Salt and black pepper				
Spinach, fresh	350g	12oz	500g	1lb
Filo pastry, packet	1 x 300g		2 x 300g	
Oil for brushing				
Sesame seeds	1 tsp		2 tsp	

Fry the mince and onion in a saucepan until golden. Add the garlic, tomatoes, mint, nutmeg and seasoning. Bring to the boil, stirring. Simmer, stirring occasionally until most of the liquid has evaporated – approx 25 minutes. Wash the spinach and remove any tough stalks. Cook in a saucepan without any extra water for approx 2–3 minutes until it has wilted.

Lightly brush each sheet of filo pastry with oil and lay in overlapping layers in the Remoska, leaving enough overhanging to wrap over the top. Spoon in the meat and spinach and wrap the pastry over to enclose, scrunching it slightly. Sprinkle with sesame seeds and cook for approx 30–40 minutes until golden and crisp.

Timing is the same for the Standard and Grand.

LAMB SPICED WITH APRICOT

	Standard		Grand	
Serves	*4*		*6*	
Oil, sunflower	2 tbsp		3 tbsp	
Lamb, minced	300g	10oz	500g	1lb
Onion, finely chopped	1 medium		1 large	
Garlic clove, crushed	1		2	
Rice, easy cook	100g	4oz	225g	8oz
Cinnamon, ground	1/2 tsp		1 tsp	
Ginger, ground	1/2 tsp		1 tsp	
Apricots, dried, ready to eat	50g	2oz	100g	4oz
Raisins, seedless	50g	2oz	100g	4oz
Salt and black pepper				
Stock, vegetable, hot	300ml	10fl oz	450ml	15fl oz

In a large non-stick frying pan heat the oil and brown the meat. Remove the meat with a slotted spoon, keep warm. In the same pan, fry the onion and the garlic until soft, return the meat to the frying pan and add all other ingredients except the stock and mix thoroughly. Transfer to the Remoska and pour in the stock which should only just cover the ingredients and cook approx for 40–45 minutes.

Timing is the same for the Standard and Grand.

LAMB ROGAN JOSH

	Standard		Grand	
Serves	*3–4*		*6–8*	
Oil, vegetable	2 tbsp		4 tbsp	
Onion, finely sliced	1 medium		1 large	
Lamb, lean, diced	175g	6oz	350g	12oz
Rogan Josh Sauce, tin	1 x 283g		2 x 283g	
Water, hot				

Heat the oil for 5 minutes in the Remoska, add the onion and cook until soft and golden. Add the lamb and cook for 5 minutes. Pour in the sauce and fill the tin with the hot water and add to the Remoska, stir and cook for approx 30 minutes or until the lamb is cooked. Serve hot.

Timing is the same for the Standard and Grand.

Variation Use diced chicken instead of the lamb.

ROAST LEG OF LAMB

	Standard		Grand	
Serves	*4–5*		*6–8*	
Lamb, leg	1kg	2lb	1.5kg	3lb
Butter (melted)	25g	1oz	50g	2oz
Rosemary, fresh, sprig	1		2	
Garlic, sliced in slivers	1		2	
Salt and black pepper				
Roasting bag				
Potatoes	500g	1lb	1kg	2lb

Trim any surplus fat from the lamb, lightly brush with melted butter. Cut a number of slits in the surface of the lamb with the point of a knife and insert rosemary and garlic. Season the lamb, place in the roasting bag or wrap well in foil. Place into the Remoska and surround with small sized potatoes. Roast for approx 1–1½ hours in the Standard, 1½–2 hours in the Grand.

Carefully open the roasting bag and drain off the stock, removing any grease from the surface. Leave to rest before serving.

LAMB STEW, MORROCAN STYLE

	Standard		Grand	
Serves	4		6–8	
Oil, olive	1 tbsp		2 tbsp	
Onion, chopped	1 large		2 large	
Garlic clove, chopped	1		2	
Lamb shoulder, boned, cubed	700g	1½lb	1.5kg	3lb
Cinnamon stick	1		1	
Mustard seeds	2 tsp		3 tsp	
Tomatoes, chopped, tin	1 x 400g		2 x 400g	
Stock, lamb	150ml	5fl oz	300ml	10fl oz
Salt and black pepper				
Saffron threads	2–3		3–4	
Turnip, cubed	100g	4oz	250g	9oz
Prunes, stoned, halved	6		15	

Heat the oil in the Remoska and cook the onion and garlic until they are soft. Add the lamb, stir and cook until it is no longer pink. Stir in the cinnamon stick, the mustard seeds, tomatoes, stock and season. Cook for approx 1 hour. Add the saffron, the turnip, and cook for a further 20 minutes. Add the prunes and cook for another 20 minutes or until the lamb and turnips are tender.

Timing is the same for the Standard and Grand.

LANCASHIRE HOT POT

	Standard		Grand	
Serves	4		6–8	
Lamb chops	8–10		12–14	
Mushrooms, sliced	100g	4oz	300g	10oz
Onions, sliced	225g	8oz	400g	14oz
Potatoes, thickly sliced	500g	1lb	1kg	2lb
Salt and black pepper				
Stock, lamb	450ml	15fl oz	1l	32fl oz
Butter	50g	2oz	100g	4oz

Remove any excess fat from the chops and lay them in the Remoska. Cover the meat with the mushrooms, then the onions and lastly the potatoes, seasoning each layer as you go. Pour over enough of the stock to just come to the top of the potatoes. Dot the top with butter. Cook for approx 90 minutes until the meat is tender. If the top is cooking too quickly make a 'foil lid' with a few layers of foil to fit inside the Remoska to cover the food, this will slow down the cooking.

Timing is the same for the Standard and Grand.

MEATBALLS

	Standard		Grand	
Serves	*4*		*8*	
Beef, pork or lamb, minced	500g	1lb	1kg	2lb
Breadcrumbs, fresh	8 tbsp		12 tbsp	
Egg	1		2	
Nutmeg, fresh, grated				
Oil, vegetable	1 tbsp		3 tbsp	
Tomato sauce, jar	1 x 300g		2 x 300g	

Mix together the meat, breadcrumbs, egg and nutmeg and with damp hands form meatballs approx 3 cm (1in) diameter. Leave to rest for 1 hour in the refrigerator. Heat the oil in the Remoska, add the meatballs and turn them with a wooden spoon to coat, cover and cook for approx 20–30 minutes, turning once or twice, until crispy and brown. Add the jar of tomato sauce, gently stir and cook for a further 10 minutes.

Timing is the same for the Standard and Grand.

MINCE WITH GARLIC BREAD

	Standard		Grand	
Serves	4		6–8	
Beef, minced	500g	1lb	700g	1¹/₂lb
Oil, olive	1 tbsp		2 tbsp	
Onion, finely chopped	1 large		2 large	
Garlic clove, crushed	1		2	
Salt and black pepper				
Pasta sauce, herb and tomato, jar	1 x 500g		*see below	
Topping				
French bread	6 slices		8–10 slices	
Garlic butter	50g	2oz	100g	4oz
Cheese, grated				

Heat a large non-stick frying pan until very hot and brown the mince in two or three batches. When browned, transfer the mince to the Remoska. Heat the oil in the non-stick frying pan, add the onions and garlic and cook until soft and golden brown. Season lightly. Pour the pasta sauce into the frying pan, (*if using the Grand Remoska use one and a half jars of sauce), mix to combine and then pour over the mince and stir. Cook for approx 30 minutes or until the mince is tender.

Topping
Meanwhile, prepare the garlic bread – spread each slice of bread generously with garlic butter and sprinkle with grated cheese. Place the bread on top of the mince. Cook until the cheese is melted and golden brown.

Timing is the same for the Standard and Grand.

Milena's Tip

Tenderise mince by mixing with a little cold water, milk, wine or beer and leave to stand for half an hour before adding seasoning and any other ingredients.

PORK & APPLE HOT POT

	Standard		Grand	
Serves	*2–3*		*6–8*	
Salt and black pepper				
Flour, plain	2 tbsp		3 tbsp	
Pork, belly, cubed	500g	1lb	1kg	2lb
Oil	1 tbsp		2 tbsp	
Butter	50g	2oz	75g	3oz
Apple, dessert, wedges	1		2	
Onion, chopped	1 large		2 large	
Tomatoes, peeled, chopped	3		5	
Potatoes, diced	500g	1lb	1kg	2lb
Stock, pork	as required		as required	

Season the flour and coat the pork cubes lightly. Heat the oil in a non-stick frying pan, brown the meat a few pieces at a time and set aside. Add the butter to the pan, cook and lightly brown the apple wedges, remove with a slotted spoon, add the onion and brown.

Transfer the onion, apple and pork to the Remoska, cover with the tomatoes and potatoes, season. Add enough hot stock to just come to the top of the potatoes but no more. Cover with buttered paper or buttered foil and cook for approx 1 hour. Remove the paper or foil and cook until the potatoes are brown.

Timing is the same for the Standard and Grand.

Milena's Tip

Turn meat with wooden spoons, to avoid scratching the Remoska and piercing the meat.

PORK CHOPS WITH APRICOTS

	Standard		Grand	
Serves	*4*		*6–8*	
Oil, olive	2 tbsp		3 tbsp	
Onion, finely sliced	1		2	
Pepper, yellow, finely sliced	1		2	
Curry powder, medium	2 tsp		4 tsp	
Flour, plain	1 tbsp		2 tbsp	
Pork chops	4		6–8	
Salt and black pepper				
Mustard, wholegrain	2 tbsp		4 tbsp	
Stock, chicken	450ml	15fl oz	1l	32fl oz
Apricots, dried	100g	4oz	175g	6oz
Cream, single	4 tbsp		6 tbsp	

Put the oil, onions and peppers into the Remoska, and cook until golden. Mix together the curry powder and flour and put to one side. Trim any excess fat off the chops, season and brown on both sides in a dry non-stick frying pan. Stir the mustard into the stock. When the onions and peppers are ready, stir in the curry powder, flour mixture and stock and add the chops and apricots. Cook for approx 30–40 minutes or until the chops are cooked through. Remove the chops to a warm serving dish, stir the cream into the sauce and pour over the chops.

Timing is the same for the Standard and Grand.

Milena's Tip

Ice cubes will remove fat from soups and stews. Just drop a few into the pan and stir, any fat will cling to the ice cubes, remove and discard before they melt!

PORK CHOPS WITH PRUNE & APPLE STUFFING

	Standard		Grand	
Serves	*4*		*8*	
Stuffing				
Prunes	100g	4oz	200g	7oz
Apple, peeled and cored	1		2	
Lemon, juice	4 tsp		8 tsp	
Sugar, brown	25g	1oz	50g	2oz
Water	1 tsp		2 tsp	
Pork chops, thick	4		8	
Salt and black pepper				
Potatoes, thinly sliced	500g	1lb	1kg	2lb
Butter	50g	2oz	100g	4oz
Stock, chicken	125ml	5fl oz	300ml	10fl oz

Stuffing
Soak the prunes in boiling water for 5 minutes and drain. Chop the prunes and apple into small pieces, and in a small saucepan cook with the lemon juice, sugar and water until slightly soft. Cool.

Bone the chops, and cut a pocket into the bone side almost to the flat end of each chop. Stuff the chops with the prune and apple mixture and place in the Remoska and season. Cover with the potatoes, dot with butter. Pour over the stock and cook for approx 1 hour until the chops are tender.

Timing is the same for the Standard and Grand.

PORK STROGANOFF

	Standard		Grand	
Serves	*4*		*6–8*	
Oil, vegetable	2 tbsp		4 tbsp	
Onion, finely sliced	1 large		2 large	
Garlic cloves, crushed	2		3–4	
Pork fillet cut into 1cm (1/2in) thick pieces	350g	12oz	500g	1lb
Flour, plain	25g	1oz	40g	11/2oz
Tomato purée	2 tbsp		4 tbsp	
Stock, chicken or vegetable, hot	400ml	14fl oz	600ml	20fl oz
Mushrooms, button, sliced	125g	5oz	250g	9oz
Pepper, green, deseeded and sliced	1		2	
Nutmeg, fresh, ground	1/2 tsp		1 tsp	
Salt and black pepper				
Sour cream or natural yogurt	4 tbsp		6–8 tbsp	

Put half of the oil, the onions and the garlic into the Remoska and cook for approx 15–20 minutes until soft and golden. Heat the remaining oil in a non-stick frying pan and brown the slices of pork. Add the flour and tomato purée to the onions and mix well to combine, and then add the stock, stirring all the time to blend thoroughly. Add the browned pork, mushrooms, pepper and nutmeg and season to taste. Cook for approx 25 minutes, stir and continue cooking for 15 minutes or until the pork is cooked. Stir in the sour cream or yogurt.

Timing is the same for the Standard and Grand.

Pork Fillet Stuffed with Apple and Pink Grapefruit

PORK FILLET STUFFED WITH APPLE & PINK GRAPEFRUIT

	Standard		Grand	
Serves	4		8	
Pork tenderloin	1 x 700g	1¹/₂ lb	2 x 700g	3lb
Apples, peeled and cored	4		8	
Grapefruit, pink	2		4	
Herbs, dried, mixed, chopped	1 tsp		2 tsp	
Breadcrumbs	100g	4oz	200g	7oz
Salt and black pepper				
Oil	2 tbsp		4 tbsp	
Vegetables, mixed	225g	8oz	500g	1lb
String				

Cut the tenderloin lengthways without cutting through the bottom, and beat out with a meat mallet or rolling pin. Cut the apples into 2¹/₂cm (1in) size pieces. Peel and segment the grapefruit. Add the herbs, the apples and the grapefruit to the bread-crumbs, season and mix well. Place the mixture in the centre of the flattened pork and roll up. Tie with string. Heat 1 tablespoon of oil in a non-stick frying pan and brown the pork all over. Put the remaining oil and vegetables in the Remoska and cook for approx 15 minutes, add the browned pork and cook for approx 35–40 minutes. Allow to cool and remove the string before slicing and serving.

When using the Grand, cook for approx 40–45 minutes.

PORK WITH PARSLEY COBBLER

	Standard		Grand	
Serves	*4*		*6–8*	
Pork loin, diced	500g	1lb	1kg	2lb
Carrots, sliced	2		4	
Swede, sliced	1		2	
Parsnips, sliced	2		3	
Leeks, sliced	2		3	
Celery sticks, sliced	2		3	
Tomato purée	2 tbsp		4 tbsp	
Parsley, fresh, chopped	2 tbsp		4 tbsp	
Pearl barley	2 tbsp		4 tbsp	
Stock, beef	600ml	20fl oz	1l	32fl oz
Celery salt and black pepper				
Topping				
Flour, plain	125g	5oz	300g	10oz
Baking powder	1 tsp		2 tsp	
Salt and black pepper				
Fromage frais, low fat	6 tbsp		12 tbsp	
Parsley, fresh, chopped	3 tbsp		6 tbsp	
Water, cold				

Dry fry the pork in a non-stick frying pan until lightly browned. Add the vegetables and stir over a medium heat until lightly coloured. Place in the Remoska and stir in the tomato purée, parsley, pearl barley and half the stock. Season with celery salt and pepper and cook for approx 30–40 minutes. Add the remaining stock and cook for approx 40–45 minutes more, or until the pork and vegetables are tender.

Topping
Sift the flour and baking powder with the seasoning, stir in the fromage frais and parsley with enough cold water to mix to a soft dough. Roll out to about 1cm ($\frac{1}{2}$in) thickness and cut into 12–16 triangles. Arrange the triangles over the casserole, overlapping if necessary. Cook for approx 20–25 minutes until well risen and golden.

Timing is the same for the Standard and Grand.

PORK TENDERLOIN IN CHINESE SAUCE

	Standard		Grand	
Serves	4		8	
Pork, fillet, thinly sliced	500g	1lb	1kg	2lb
Garlic cloves, crushed	2		4	
Ginger, fresh, peeled, sliced	3cm	1¹/₂in	5cm	2in
Honey	3 tsp		1 tbsp	
Soy sauce, light	3 tsp		1 tbsp	
Sherry, dry	1 tbsp		3 tbsp	
Oil, sesame	2 tbsp		2 tbsp	
Yellow bean sauce	4 tsp		2 tbsp	
Sesame seeds, toasted	4 tsp		2 tbsp	

Use the Shallow Pan.

Place the pork in a single layer in the Remoska. Combine all the remaining ingredients except the sesame seeds in a saucepan and heat through, mix well. Pour over the pork and spread evenly. Cook for approx 30–40 minutes, or until tender, basting 2 or 3 times. Sprinkle with the sesame seeds when serving.

Timing is the same for the Standard and Grand.

SAUSAGE & APPLE PIE

	Standard or Grand	
Serves	6	
Shortcrust pastry	300g	10oz
Sausage, Cumberland	225g	8oz
Butter	15g	1oz
Apples, dessert, cored and diced	2	
Egg yolks	2	
Egg	1	
Cream, whipping	250ml	8fl oz
Cheese, Lancashire, diced	50g	2oz

Line an 18cm x 4cm (8in x 1¹/₂in) loose bottom baking tin with the pastry, prick the base with a fork and cook in the Remoska for approx 20 minutes. Remove the skin from the sausages and fry in a dry non-stick frying pan until cooked. Drain on kitchen paper. In a small saucepan melt the butter and cook the apples until soft but holding shape. Mix the egg yolks and egg with the cream. Place the cooked sausage in an even layer in the pastry shell, add the apples and pour over the egg and cream. Dot with the cheese and cook for approx 25–35 minutes until golden brown and slightly firm to the touch.

Timing is the same for the Standard and Grand.

SAUSAGE MEAT MOUSSAKA

	Standard		Grand	
Serves	*4*		*6*	
Butter or Margarine	50g	2oz	75g	3oz
Onion, thinly sliced	1 large		1¹/₂ large	
Sausage Meat	500g	1lb	700g	1¹/₂lb
Sage, dried	1 tsp		1¹/₂ tsp	
Thyme, dried	¹/₂ tsp		1 tsp	
Garlic clove, crushed	1		2	
Tomatoes, tin	1 x 400g		*see below	
Salt and black pepper				
Potatoes, sliced	500g	1lb	700g	1¹/₂lb
Apples, Bramleys, cored, peeled, sliced	225g	8oz	300g	10oz
Cheese sauce	600ml	20fl oz	1l	32fl oz

In a large non-stick frying pan melt the butter or margarine and fry the onion until soft. Stir in the sausage meat and fry gently for 10 minutes – stirring. Remove from the heat, drain off excess fat, stir in the sage, thyme, garlic and tomatoes (*if using the Grand Remoska use one and a half tins of tomatoes) and season to taste.

Place half the potatoes and all the apples in the Remoska, add the sausage meat mixture, cover with the rest of the potatoes.

Make a cheese sauce (see page 182). Pour over the potatoes and cook for approx 40 minutes until the potatoes are cooked.

Timing is the same for the Standard and Grand.

SAUSAGE & NEW POTATO BAKE

	Standard		Grand	
Serves	*4*		*8*	
Sausages	500g	1lb	1kg	2lb
Potatoes, new	700g	1¹/₂lb	1.5kg	3lb
Onion, red, roughly chopped	1		2	
Onion, white, roughly chopped	2		3	
Oil, olive	2 tsp		1 tbsp	
Black pepper				
Cheese, Cheddar, grated	100g	4oz	200g	7oz

Cut each sausage into three and thickly slice the potatoes. Mix together with the onions and oil. Lightly season with black pepper (the sausages will add seasoning). Place in the Remoska and cook for approx 45–60 minutes, stirring once or twice. Finally sprinkle on the cheese, replace the lid, switch off and leave for a few minutes. The heat will melt the cheese. Serve immediately.

Timing is the same for the Standard and Grand.

SAUSAGE PIE

	Standard		Grand	
Serves	*4*		*6–8*	
Sausages	500g	1lb	1kg	2lb
Oil	2 tbsp		4 tbsp	
Onion, sliced	1		2	
Tomatoes, skinned	300g	10oz	500g	1lb
Worcestershire sauce	1/2 tsp		1 tsp	
Potatoes	500g	1lb	1kg	2lb
Milk	100ml	4fl oz	300ml	10fl oz
Butter or margarine	25g	1oz	75g	3oz
Salt and black pepper				
Parsley, fresh, chopped	1 tbsp		2 tbsp	

Heat the oil in a non-stick frying pan and fry the sausages. Retain two for decoration, and skin the others. Cut in half lengthways and place into the Remoska. Fry the onion in the same frying pan, add the quartered tomatoes and Worcestershire sauce. Stir and pour this mixture over the sausages.

In a saucepan cook the potatoes. Drain and mash the potatoes with the milk and butter. Season to taste. Cover the sausage mixture with the potato mash, forking the top. Slice the 2 whole sausages and arrange them around the edge. Dot with a little butter and cook for approx 30–40 minutes, until the potato starts to brown. Sprinkle with parsley and serve.

Timing is the same for the Standard and Grand.

Milena's Tip

If you are without a mortar and pestle, crush black peppercorns by placing in a polythene bag and roll firmly on a solid surface with a rolling pin.

SAUSAGE & BUTTERNUT SQUASH BAKE

	Standard		Grand	
Serves	*4*		*8–10*	
Sausages, Lincolnshire	400g	14oz	1kg	2lb
Butternut squash	1		2	
Sweet potatoes	1–2		2–3	
Onion, peeled and sliced into rings	1		2	
Sage, fresh, chopped	1 tbsp		2 tbsp	
Oil, olive	1 tbsp		2 tbsp	
Salt and black pepper				

Slice each sausage into 2 or 3 pieces and put into a bowl. Peel the butternut squash and sweet potatoes, slice into 2 cm (1in) pieces. Add the onion and sage, oil, salt and black pepper, mix and transfer to the Remoska. Cook for approx 40–60 minutes, stirring the dish once or twice.

Timing is the same for the Standard and Grand.

SAUSAGE & ROOT VEGETABLE BAKE

	Standard		Grand	
Serves	*4–6*		*8–10*	
Sausages, Cumberland	700g	1$^{1}/_{2}$lb	1.25kg	2$^{1}/_{2}$lb
Oil, olive	1–2 tbsp		3 tbsp	
Onion, finely chopped	1		2	
Celeriac, roughly grated	1		1$^{1}/_{2}$	
Swede, roughly grated	1		2	
Turnip, roughly grated	1		2	
Potatoes, roughly grated	2 medium		4 medium	
Parsnips, roughly grated	2		4	
Sage leaves	2–3		3–4	
Black pepper				

Brown the sausages in a non-stick frying pan with a little of the oil and put to one side. Brown the onions in the frying pan. Add the rest of the vegetables coating them well in the oil and add the sage leaves. Season with freshly ground black pepper. Transfer to the Remoska, place the sausages on top and cook for approx 35–45 minutes until the sausages are cooked.

Timing is the same for the Standard and Grand.

TOULOUSE SAUSAGE & LENTIL CASSEROLE

	Standard		Grand	
Serves	*4*		*8*	
Lentils, green or brown	300g	10oz	500g	1lb
Oil, olive	2 tbsp		4 tbsp	
Onions, chopped	2		4	
Celery sticks, chopped	3		5	
Garlic cloves, crushed	2		3	
Thyme, fresh, sprigs	3		5	
Bay leaf	1		2	
Tomatoes, peeled, chopped	3 large		6 large	
Tomato purée	2 tsp		1 tbsp	
Wine, red	200ml	7fl oz	400ml	14fl oz
Water (see below)				
Toulouse or other sausages	700g	1¹/₂lb	1.5kg	3lb
Parsley, fresh, flat leaf	1 bunch		1 bunch	

Soak the lentils according to the package. It may be overnight but some varieties do not need that long. Drain them and set aside. In the Remoska heat the oil, add the onions, celery and garlic and cook for 10 minutes. Add thyme (stripped from the stalks), bay leaf, tomatoes and purée and cook for approx 7–10 minutes. Add the lentils and wine and enough water just to cover. Place the sausages on top and cook for approx 30–40 minutes. Garnish with chopped parsley.

Timing is the same for the Standard or Grand.

Milena's Tip

Remember, do not heat an empty Remoska. Place a bowl of water in the Remoska for about five minutes if you want to pre-heat before adding the ingredients.

Veal Olives Stuffed with Shallots and Black Cherries

VEAL OLIVES STUFFED WITH SHALLOTS & BLACK CHERRIES

	Standard		Grand	
Serves	*4*		*6*	
Veal slices, thin	8		12	
Shallots	350g	12oz	500g	1lb
Oil	2 tbsp		3 tbsp	
Onion, sliced	50g	2oz	100g	4oz
Tomatoes, cherry	100g	4oz	200g	7oz
Cherries, black, stoned	125g	5oz	300g	10oz
Worcestershire sauce	1 tsp		2 tsp	
Stuffing mix, sage and onion	50g	2oz	100g	4oz
Salt and black pepper				
String or cocktail sticks				

Beat the veal slices thinly with a meat mallet or rolling pin. Cover with cling film and place in the refrigerator. Cut the tops off the shallots and simmer in water for 10 minutes (skins may be left on as they will be easier to peel when cooked). Heat the oil in the Remoska, add the onions and cook for approx 10 minutes. Add the tomatoes and cook for a further 5 minutes. Meanwhile, peel the shallots and cut in half or quarters if large. Mix with the cherries, Worcestershire sauce, stuffing mix and seasoning.

Lay out the flattened veal slices. Divide and spread the filling onto the centre of the veal slices. Roll each one up and tie with string or use cocktail sticks. Place on top of the onion and tomatoes in the Remoska and cook for approx 30–40 minutes. Cool slightly, remove the string before serving.

Timing is the same for the Standard and Grand.

&SEA

FISH
FOOD

Fish and seafood can be cooked in the Remoska in hardly any time at all to provide a nutritious meal.

COD COBBLER

	Standard		Grand	
Serves	4		8	
Butter for greasing				
Cod fillets, skinless	700g	1¹/₂lb	1.5kg	3lb
Cheese sauce	450ml	15fl oz	900ml	1¹/₂pt
Scones				
Butter	50g	2oz	100g	4oz
Flour, plain	225g	8oz	400g	14oz
Baking powder	1 tsp		2 tsp	
Salt	¹/₄ tsp		¹/₂ tsp	
Cheese, Cheddar, grated	50g	2oz	100g	4oz
Egg, yolk	1		2	
Milk (see below)				

Place cod fillets in the bottom of the greased Remoska. Make the cheese sauce (see page 182) and pour over the fish.
Scones
Rub the butter into the flour adding the baking powder and the salt. Mix in most of the cheese with the egg yolk into the mixture with enough milk to make a soft dough. Roll out to a thickness of 2cm (¹/₂ in) and cut into small rounds with a scone cutter. Place the scone rounds on top of the sauce just covering the surface. Glaze with milk, sprinkle the remaining cheese over the scones. Cook for approx 25–30 minutes or until the scones are golden brown. There are scone mixes available in most supermarkets.

Timing is the same for the Standard and Grand.

COD WITH CRUNCHY TOPPING

	Standard		Grand	
Serves	4		8	
Cod, pieces, skinned	4 x 125g	4 x 5oz	8 x 125g	8 x 5oz
Tomatoes, sliced	2		4	
Breadcrumbs, wholemeal	50g	2oz	100g	4oz
Parsley, fresh, chopped	2 tbsp		2 tbsp	
Lemon, zest and juice	¹/₂		1	
Oil	1 tsp		1 tbsp	
Salt and black pepper				

Arrange the cod in the Remoska. Cover with tomatoes. Mix together the breadcrumbs, parsley, lemon zest and juice, oil and seasoning. Spoon the crumb mixture evenly over the fish and cook for approx 25–35 minutes until the fish is cooked and the top crispy.

Timing is the same for the Standard and Grand.

COD WITH MEDITERRANEAN TOPPING

	Standard		Grand	
Serves	*4*		*8*	
Oil, olive	1 tbsp		2 tbsp	
Onion, chopped	1 medium		2 medium	
Peppers, red, roughly diced	2		4	
Garlic clove, crushed	1		2	
Tomatoes, chopped, tin	1 x 400g		2 x 400g	
Tomato purée	1 tbsp		2 tbsp	
Sugar, brown	1/4 tsp		1/2 tsp	
Salt and black pepper				
Cod fillets	4 x 175g	4 x 6oz	8 x 175g	8 x 6oz
Olives, black, stoned	8		16	
Parsley, fresh, chopped				

Heat the oil in a non-stick frying pan, cook the onion and peppers until softened. Add the garlic and cook for another 2–3 minutes. Add the tomatoes, tomato purée, sugar and seasoning. Cook over a low to medium heat for 30 minutes, stirring occasionally, or until the mixture is rich and has a thick sauce consistency.

Pat the cod fillets dry and place skin-side down in the Remoska. Spoon the sauce on top of each fillet and scatter the olives on top. Cook for approx 15–20 minutes or until the cod is cooked through. Serve garnished with parsley.

Timing is the same for the Standard and Grand.

COD RAREBIT

	Standard		Grand	
Serves	*3*		*5*	
Butter for greasing				
Cheese, Cheddar, Lancashire or Gruyère, grated	225g	8oz	350g	12oz
Mustard, Dijon	1 tbsp		2 tbsp	
Cream, single	3 tbsp		5 tbsp	
Cod steaks	3 x 175g	3 x 6oz	5 x 175g	5 x 6oz
Salt and black pepper				

Lightly grease the Remoska with butter. Mix together the cheese, mustard and cream and spread evenly over the cod. Put the cod steaks into the Remoska and season to taste. Cook for 20–25 minutes until the topping is brown and bubbling and the fish is cooked.

Timing is the same for the Standard and Grand.

COD WITH MUSHROOMS

	Standard		Grand	
Serves	*4*		*8*	
Oil for greasing				
Cod fillets	500g	1lb	700g	1¹/₂ lb
Mushroom soup, tin, concentrated	1 x 295g		2 x 295g	
Milk	2 tbsp		4 tbsp	
Sherry, dry	2 tbsp		3 tbsp	
Cayenne pepper	¹/₂ tsp		³/₄ tsp	
Mustard powder	¹/₂ tsp		1 tsp	
Salt and black pepper				

Place the fish into the greased Remoska. Heat the soup in a saucepan, stirring in the milk, sherry, cayenne pepper, mustard and season to taste. Pour over the fish and cook for approx 25–30 minutes.

Timing is the same for the Standard and Grand.

FISH & CHEESE FLAN

	Standard	
Serves	*4*	
Pastry case, 18cm (7in)		
Cream, double	2 tbsp	
Egg	2	
Cheese, cottage	100g	4oz
Salmon or tuna, tin	1 x 175g	
Béchamel sauce	450ml	15fl oz
Tomatoes, sliced	1–2	
Butter for brushing		
Salt and black pepper		

Buy a flan case or bake one in the usual way but keep in your baking tin. Add the cream, 1 whole egg and 1 egg yolk, the cottage cheese and the drained flaked fish to the Béchamel sauce (see page 180). Fold in the stiffly beaten egg white. Turn the mixture into the pastry case and cook in the Remoska for approx 30 minutes. 10 minutes before the end, arrange thinly sliced tomatoes around the edge and brush with a little melted butter. Season.

FISH GRATIN

	Standard		Grand	
Serves	*4*		*6–8*	
Fish, mixed – cod, haddock, hake, plaice, cut into strips	700g	1¹/₂lb	1.25kg	2¹/₂lb
Lemon juice (see below)				
Prawns	100g	4oz	250g	9oz
Mushrooms, finely sliced	50g	2oz	125g	5oz
Béchamel sauce	400ml	14fl oz	600ml	20fl oz
Cheese, Parmesan, grated	50g	2oz	125g	5oz

Lay the fish strips in the Remoska and sprinkle with lemon juice. Cover with the prawns and mushrooms. Cover with warm Béchamel sauce (see page 180), sprinkle with cheese and cook for approx 30–40 minutes until pale gold.

Timing is the same for the Standard and Grand.

FISH HOT POT

Serves	Standard		Grand	
	4		6–8	
Fish, haddock or cod	500g	1lb	1kg	2lb
Onions, thinly sliced	50g	2oz	175g	6oz
Beans, French	100g	4oz	175g	6oz
Cheese, Cheddar, grated	100g	4oz	175g	6oz
Salt and black pepper				
Tomatoes, sliced	250g	9oz	500g	1lb
Potatoes, thinly sliced	500g	1lb	1kg	2lb
Stock, fish	150ml	5fl oz	300ml	10fl oz
Butter, melted				

Skin the fish, cut into 5cm (1½in) pieces and put into the Remoska. Cover with onions, beans, half the grated cheese and season. Cover with tomatoes and overlapping potatoes. Season lightly, pour in the stock and brush the potatoes with melted butter. Cook for approx 40–60 minutes. Sprinkle with the remaining cheese, season lightly and continue cooking until brown, approx 10 minutes.

Timing is the same for the Standard and Grand.

MOROCCAN STYLE FISH

Serves	Standard		Grand	
	4		8	
Garlic clove, crushed	1		2	
Cumin, ground	2 tbsp		3 tbsp	
Paprika, sweet	2 tbsp		3 tbsp	
Tomato purée	2 tbsp		3 tbsp	
Lemon, juice	2 tbsp		4 tbsp	
Whiting or cod cutlets	4 x 175g	4 x 6oz	8 x 175g	8 x 6oz
Tomatoes, sliced	350g	12oz	500g	1lb
Peppers, green, thinly sliced	2		3	
Salt and black pepper				
Parsley, fresh, chopped				

Mix together the garlic, cumin, paprika, tomato purée and lemon juice. Spread the mixture over the fish, cover and chill for 30 minutes to marinate. Arrange half the tomatoes and peppers in the base of the Remoska. Cover with the fish, then arrange the remaining tomatoes and peppers on top. Season. Cover with foil and cook for approx 45 minutes until the fish is tender. Sprinkle with parsley to serve.

Timing is the same for Standard and Grand.

BAKED HALIBUT

	Standard		Grand	
Serves	*3*		*6*	
Butter, melted	1 tbsp		1 tbsp	
Halibut fillets	3		6	
Onion, sliced	1 medium		2 medium	
Parsley, fresh, chopped	4 tbsp		6 tbsp	
Tomato juice	250ml	8fl oz	450ml	15fl oz
Salt and black pepper				

Brush the Remoska with butter and add the fish. Arrange the onion slices on top and sprinkle with half the parsley. Pour on the tomato juice, season well. Cook for approx 30 minutes or until the fish is cooked. Sprinkle with the remaining parsley and serve hot.

Timing is the same for the Standard and Grand.

MACKEREL WITH LEMON & THYME

	Standard	Grand
Serves	*4*	*6*
Oil, olive as needed		
Mackerel fillets, medium	4	6
Salt and black pepper		
Lemon, zest and juice	1	2
Thyme, leaves, fresh	2 tsp	3 tsp

Lightly oil the Remoska and put in the mackerel fillets, then season to taste. Sprinkle over the zest and juice from the lemon. Leave for an hour, turning the fillets occasionally. Drizzle the fillets with a little olive oil and add the thyme. Cook for approx 20 minutes or until the fillets are cooked.

Timing is the same for the Standard and Grand.

PLAICE WITH DILL

	Standard		Grand	
Serves	1–2		2–4	
Butter	25g	1oz	50g	2oz
Plaice, whole, cleaned and trimmed	1 large		2 large	
Salt and black pepper				
Lemon, zest and juice	1		2	
Dill, fresh, chopped	1 tbsp		2 tbsp	

Lightly grease the Remoska with half the butter. Make three slashes on both sides of the fish. Season both the skin side of the fish and the cavity, and then sprinkle a little lemon zest and chopped dill into the cavity. Place the fish into the Remoska. Dot with the remaining butter and squeeze over the juice of half the lemon. Cook for approx 20–30 minutes or until the fish is cooked. Sprinkle with dill and a little more lemon juice (optional).

Timing is the same for the Standard and Grand.

PRAWN & ASPARAGUS QUICHE

	Standard or Grand	
Serves	4	
Flan case, bought, 18cm (7in)		
Prawns	100g	4oz
Asparagus tips, tin	1 x 350g	
Eggs	3	
Salt and black pepper		
Cream, double	300ml	10fl oz

Lay the prawns in the flan case. Place about two thirds of the drained asparagus over the top. Whisk the eggs with salt and plenty of black pepper and mix with the cream. Pour over the prawns and asparagus. Cook in the Remoska for approx 20 minutes, add the remaining asparagus, pushing them into the mixture a little to prevent them from drying out, continue cooking until the quiche has set and has turned a golden colour.

Use either the Standard or Grand to bake the same size quiche.

PRAWNS WITH SPICED RICE

	Standard		Grand	
Serves	*4*		*6–8*	
Oil, vegetable	1 tbsp		2 tbsp	
Turmeric, ground	1/2 tbsp		1 tbsp	
Paprika, sweet	1/2 tbsp		1 tbsp	
Ginger, ground	1/2 tbsp		1 tbsp	
Rice, long grain	150ml	5fl oz	300ml	10fl oz
Peas, frozen, defrosted	175g	6oz	350g	12oz
Stock, vegetable, hot	300ml	10fl oz	600ml	20fl oz
Salt and black pepper				
Prawns, defrosted if frozen	175g	6oz	350g	12oz

Put the oil, turmeric, paprika and ginger into the Remoska. Cook for 15 minutes. Add the rice, peas and stock, and stir to blend with the spices. Cook for approx 20–25 minutes or until the rice is cooked. Season to taste. Add the prawns, stir in and cook for 5 minutes. Serve hot.

Timing is the same for the Standard and Grand.

PRAWNS & TUNA WITH PASTA

	Standard		Grand	
Serves	*4–6*		*6–8*	
Oil, olive	1 tbsp		2 tbsp	
Spring onions, finely sliced	1 bunch		2 bunches	
Mushrooms, chestnut, sliced	175g	6oz	250g	9oz
Pasta, Penne	125g	5oz	250g	9oz
Cornflour	2 tbsp		3 tbsp	
Milk	450ml	15fl oz	600ml	20fl oz
Salt and black pepper				
Nutmeg, fresh, grated				
Tuna, tin	2 x 175g		3 x 175g	
Prawns, cooked	225g	8oz	400g	14oz
Breadcrumbs, fresh, white	50g	2oz	100g	4oz
Cheese, Cheddar, grated	100g	4oz	175g	6oz

Put the oil, onions and mushrooms into the Remoska and cook for approx 15 minutes. Cook the pasta according to the packet instructions and drain. Mix the cornflour with a little of the milk until smooth. In a saucepan, heat the remaining milk and stir in the cornflour mixture, then bring slowly to the boil, stirring until thickened and smooth, making a white sauce. Season with salt, black pepper and nutmeg. Add the cooked pasta, white sauce, the drained tuna and prawns to the Remoska, stir lightly to combine. Sprinkle the mixture with the breadcrumbs and cheese. Cook for approx 25–30 minutes until the top is golden brown. Serve hot.

Timing is the same for the Standard and Grand.

SALMON & ASPARAGUS IN PASTRY

	Standard		Grand	
Serves	*2*		*4*	
Asparagus, fresh	175g	6oz	350g	12oz
Salmon fillet	2 x 125g	2 x 5oz	4 x 125g	4 x 5oz
Lemon, juice	1		2	
Salt and black pepper				
Pastry, puff	350g	12oz	500g	1lb
Egg, beaten	1		1	

Clean and trim the asparagus, simmer in a saucepan for 5 minutes and cool. Split each salmon fillet in half lengthways, squeeze the lemon juice over the fillet pieces and lightly season.

Roll out the puff pastry into 15cm (6in) by 12cm (5in) rectangles. Place one half of the fillet of salmon on the pastry, then some of the asparagus and sandwich with the other half. Lightly dampen the edges of the pastry and fold over to make a parcel. Brush with the egg, lightly score the top and cook in the Remoska for approx 20–30 minutes or until the pastry is risen and pale gold.

Timing is the same for the Standard and Grand.

Salmon and Asparagus in Pastry

Salmon with Coriander and Lime

SALMON WITH CORIANDER & LIME

	Standard	Grand
Serves	*4*	*6*
Salmon fillet	4 pieces	6 pieces
Lime, finely grated zest and juice	1	2
Honey, runny	2 tbsp	3 tbsp
Ginger, fresh, grated	2 tbsp	3 tbsp
Oil, olive	1 tbsp	2 tbsp
Coriander, fresh, finely chopped	2 tbsp	3 tbsp

Put the pieces of salmon skin side down in the Remoska. Mix together the lime zest and juice, honey, ginger, oil and coriander. Pour over the salmon and leave for 10–15 minutes. Cook for approx 15–20 minutes, depending on the thickness of the salmon fillets.

Serve hot or warm.

Timing is the same for the Standard and Grand.

SALMON FISH CAKES WITH CHILLI SALSA

	Standard		Grand	
Serves	*4*		*8*	
Salsa				
Tomatoes, ripe, diced small	250g	9oz	500g	1lb
Onion, red, finely chopped	1 small		2 small	
Chilli, red, deseeded and finely chopped	1		2	
Cucumber, diced small	6cm	2¹/₂in	12cm	5in
Lime, juice	1		2	
Salt and black pepper				
Fish Cakes				
Potatoes, peeled, diced large	400g	14oz	700g	1¹/₂lb
Salmon fillet	400g	14oz	700g	1¹/₂lb
Mayonnaise, low fat	1¹/₂ tbsp		3 tbsp	
Fromage frais	1¹/₂ tbsp		3 tbsp	
Basil pesto	2 tsp		1 tbsp	
Chilli, green, finely chopped	1		1	
Coriander, fresh, chopped	1 tbsp		2 tbsp	
Salt and black pepper				
Flour, plain	as needed		as needed	
Oil, olive	1 tbsp		2 tbsp	

Use the Shallow Pan.

Salsa
Prepare the salsa first by placing all the ingredients in a bowl, stir well, cover and refrigerate until needed.

Fish Cakes
Cook the potatoes in boiling salted water until soft. Meanwhile, poach the salmon in simmering water for a few minutes until just cooked (don't overcook or the cakes will be dry). Remove and discard the skin and flake the fish, reserve.

Drain the cooked potatoes, tip into a large bowl and roughly mash, until you have some small lumps left. Stir the mayonnaise and fromage frais into the potatoes, then add the pesto, chilli, coriander and plenty of seasoning. Fold in the salmon, retaining whole flakes if possible. Sprinkle the flour onto a chopping board and make 8 fish cakes with the fish mixture, doing this as lightly as possible – you want a rustic look. Coat both sides of the cakes with flour. Brush both sides of the cakes with oil, transfer to the Remoska.

Cook for approx 20–30 minutes, or until lightly golden, turning halfway through. Serve immediately with salsa.

Timing is the same for the Standard and Grand.

SALMON PARCELS

	Standard	Grand
Serves	*4*	*8*
Salmon, red or pink, tin	1 x 180g	2 x 180g
Parsley, fresh, chopped	1 tbsp	2 tbsp
Spring onions, finely chopped	4	8
Pastry, filo, sheets	4	8
Oil for brushing		
Spring onions and salad leaves		

Drain the salmon, discarding any skin and bones. Flake with a fork and mix with the parsley and onions. Place a single sheet of filo pastry on a work surface and brush lightly with oil, keeping the other sheets covered with clingfilm to prevent drying out. Place another sheet on top. Cut into six squares about 10cm (4in). Repeat with the remaining pastry. Place 1 tablespoonful of the salmon mixture onto each square. Brush the edges of the pastry with oil and draw together, pressing to seal. Place the parcels in the Remoska and cook for approx 15–20 minutes until golden. Serve with extra spring onions and salad leaves on the side.

Timing is the same for the Standard and Grand.

SALMON KOULIBIAC

	Standard		Grand	
Serves	*4*		*8*	
Salmon, tin	1 x 450g		2 x 450g	
Salt and black pepper				
Lemon, juice	$^1/_2$		1	
Pastry, puff	500g	1lb	700g	1$^1/_2$lb
Eggs, hard boiled	4		6	
Mushrooms, small, sliced	50g	2oz	100g	4oz
Parsley, fresh, chopped	1 tbsp		3 tbsp	
Egg	1		1	

Drain, skin and bone the salmon. Flake and season with salt, plenty of black pepper and lemon juice. Roll out half the puff pastry into a circle to fit the base of the Remoska. Arrange half the salmon over the circle, add the roughly chopped hard boiled eggs, mushrooms and parsley, then top with the rest of the salmon. Brush the edge with the beaten egg and lay on another circle of puff pastry, rolled out slightly larger and marked all over with small slits made with a knife. This will help to keep it even when the puff pastry is rising. Seal the edges, using any surplus pastry to decorate the top. Brush with the beaten egg and cook in the Remoska for approx 30–40 minutes until the pastry is puffed up and brown.

Timing is the same for the Standard and Grand.

Milena's Tip

If removing the skin of fish, put a small amount of salt on the ends of your fingers, this provides you with a better grip.

SALMON SCONE RING

	Grand	
Serves	8	
Filling		
Salmon, tin	1 x 225g	
Milk (see below)		
Margarine	15g	1/2oz
Flour, plain	25g	1oz
Parsley, fresh, chopped	1 tsp	
Egg, hardboiled	1	
Salt and black pepper		
Lemon, juice	2 tsp	
Scone		
Flour, self-raising	175g	6oz
Salt	1/2 tsp	
Margarine	50g	2oz
Milk	3–4 tbsp	
Egg, beaten	1	

Filling
Drain the liquor from the salmon and make up to 150ml (5fl oz) with milk. Remove any bones and grey skin from the salmon. Melt the margarine in a saucepan, add the flour, and cook for 2–3 minutes. Add the salmon liquid and milk and cook to thicken. Add lightly flaked salmon, parsley, chopped egg, seasoning, lemon juice and bind together.

Scone
Sift together the flour and salt. Rub in the margarine. Add milk to form a soft dough. Knead lightly and roll the dough out to 36cm (15in) x 20cm (8in) and spread the salmon mixture evenly over the dough leaving a small border. Damp the long edges and roll up like a Swiss roll. Lightly grease the Remoska and curl the roll inside, don't worry if the pastry cracks. Brush with a little beaten egg or milk, make diagonal cuts at 2cm (1in) intervals along the top. Cook for approx 30 minutes until well risen and golden brown. Serve in slices either hot or cold. Excellent for buffets.

SEAFOOD LASAGNE

	Standard		Grand	
Serves	*4*		*6–8*	
Oil, olive	2 tbsp		3 tbsp	
Leek, white part only, sliced	1		2	
Tomatoes, tin	1 x 400g		2 x 400g	
Tomato purée	2 tbsp		3 tbsp	
Prawns, chopped	400g	14oz	700g	1¹/₂lb
Fish, firm white, cubed	250g	9oz	500g	1lb
Black pepper				
Lasagne, spinach sheets	8		14–16	
Cheese, Cheddar, grated	175g	6oz	350g	12oz

Heat the oil in a large non-stick frying pan and cook the leek over a medium heat to soften. Stir in the tomatoes and tomato purée and bring to the boil. Reduce the heat and simmer uncovered for approx 15 minutes, or until the sauce reduces and thickens slightly. Add the prawns and fish, cover and cook for 3–4 minutes longer. Season to taste with freshly ground black pepper.

Spread one third of the sauce over the base of the Remoska and top with enough lasagne sheets to cover. Spread another third of the sauce over and cover with the remaining lasagne sheets. Spread the remainder of the sauce over, making sure all the lasagne sheets are covered. Sprinkle the cheese over and cook for approx 35–45 minutes until the lasagne is cooked. Serve immediately.

Note Some of the prawns could be replaced with small pieces of smoked salmon, or smoked haddock.

Timing is the same for the Standard and Grand.

Milena's Tip

Fish is at its best when fresh.

When buying fish look for –

1   fish free from any strong odour

2   red gills

3   bright eyes

4   firm flesh

5   a stiff tail –

    a flabby tail is a sure sign that a fish is not fresh

TROUT BAKED WITH BACON

	Standard		Grand	
Serves	2		4	
Trout, whole, cleaned, heads and fins removed	2 x 300g	2 x 10oz	4 x 300g	4 x 10oz
Bacon, thin streaky rashers	4		8	
Parsley, fresh, chopped				

Wrap two rashers of bacon in a spiral around each fish, using cocktail sticks to secure. Place them in the Remoska. Bake for 20–25 minutes, until tender. Remove the cocktail sticks. Serve garnished with chopped parsley.

Timing is the same for the Standard and Grand.

TROUT WITH LEMON & THYME

	Standard	Grand
Serves	2	4
Oil for greasing		
Trout, whole, cleaned, heads and fins removed	2 med	4 med or 2 large
Salt and black pepper		
Lemon	1	2
Thyme, fresh, sprigs	4	8
Spring onions, finely chopped	4	4–6

Lightly oil the Remoska. Make three diagonal cuts on each side of the trout. Season and insert two slices of lemon and two sprigs of thyme in each cavity and place the trout in the Remoska. Lightly season the top of the trout. Add the onions and juice from the remaining lemon. Cook for approx 25 minutes or until the trout is cooked. Serve hot or warm.

Timing is the same for the Standard and Grand.

PASTA &RICE

Pasta is best made from durum wheat mixed with either water or eggs.

Rice contains starch which determines how different varieties behave when cooked.

FUSILLI WITH PUTTANESCA SAUCE

	Standard		Grand	
Serves	*2–3*		*4–6*	
Oil, olive	1 tbsp		2 tbsp	
Onion, finely chopped	1 medium		2 medium	
Garlic clove, crushed	1–2		2–4	
Puttanesca sauce, jar	1 x 350g		2 x 350g	
Water, warm	150ml	5fl oz	300ml	10fl oz
Pasta, Fusilli, fresh	250g	9oz	500g	1lb
Salt and black pepper				

Put the oil, onion and garlic into the Remoska and cook until soft. Add the sauce, and warm water, mix gently with the onions and garlic. Stir in the fusilli and coat with the sauce and cook for approx 10 minutes.

Timing is the same for the Standard and Grand.

LINGUINE WITH TUNA & LEMON

	Standard		Grand	
Serves	*6*		*8–10*	
Pasta, Linguine	200g	7oz	300g	10oz
Oil, olive	2 tbsp		4 tbsp	
Garlic clove, crushed	1		2	
Parsley, fresh, chopped	4 tbsp		6–8 tbsp	
Tuna in brine, tin, drained	1 x 200g		2 x 200g	
Lemon, juice	4 tbsp		6 tbsp	
Cheese, Parmesan, grated	50g	2oz	75g	3oz
Butter	2 tbsp		3 tbsp	
Salt and black pepper				

Cook the pasta according to the instructions on the packet, and then drain. Put the oil and garlic into the Remoska and cook for 8 minutes or until the garlic is golden but not browned. Add the parsley, flaked tuna, lemon juice, Parmesan and butter, and stir gently to combine. Season the sauce using more black pepper than salt and add the cooked pasta. Stir well and cook for approx 10–15 minutes to heat through.

Timing is the same for the Standard and Grand.

PENNE ARRABIATA

	Standard		Grand	
Serves	*4*		*6–8*	
Oil, olive	1 tbsp		2 tbsp	
Onion, finely chopped	1 large		2 large	
Garlic cloves	3–4		4–6	
Tomatoes, chopped, tin	2 x 400g		3 x 400g	
Tomato purée	1 tbsp		2 tbsp	
Lemon, zest, grated	1		2	
Chillies, red, fresh, sliced	3–4		4–6	
Sugar, caster	2 tsp		4 tsp	
Salt and black pepper				
Pasta, Penne, fresh	250g	9oz	500g	1lb
Breadcrumbs, white, fresh	6 tbsp		12 tbsp	
Cheese, Parmesan or Pecorino grated	4 tbsp		8 tbsp	
Butter	50g	2oz	100g	4oz

Put the oil and onions into the Remoska and cook until soft, add the garlic and cook for a further 5 minutes. Stir in the tomatoes, tomato purée, lemon zest, chillies, sugar and season to taste, cook for approx 25 minutes. Add the pasta, stir to coat with the sauce. Cook for 10 minutes. Mix together the breadcrumbs and cheese and sprinkle over the pasta and sauce. Dot with the butter and cook for approx 10 minutes or until golden brown.

Timing is the same for the Standard and Grand.

Milena's Tip

When using pasta you can mix different types in the same recipe to add interest. For example use ordinary and green tagliatelle or lasagne in the same dish.

RED PEPPERS WITH PASTA STUFFING

	Standard		Grand	
Serves	6		8–10	
Pasta, Conchigliette	100g	4oz	200g	7oz
Peppers, red	6		8–10	
Salt and black pepper				
Oil, olive (see below)				
Olives, black, sliced, tin	1 x 185g		2 x 185g	
Parsley, fresh, chopped	4 tbsp		6–8 tbsp	
Basil, fresh, chopped	2 tbsp		4 tbsp	
Garlic cloves, crushed	2		4	
Anchovies, chopped, tin	2 x 50g		3 x 50g	
Capers, drained	1 tsp		2 tsp	
Cheese, Mozzarella, finely diced	200g	7oz	400g	14oz

Cook the pasta according to the instructions on the packet, and then drain. Cut the tops off the peppers and retain. Remove the seeds, being careful not to pierce the peppers, then sprinkle the insides with salt and pepper and a little oil. Mix together the olives, parsley, basil, garlic, anchovies, capers and mozzarella. Add the cooked pasta and mix well, then fill the peppers. Place in the Remoska, if necessary using some aluminium foil to ensure that they stand firmly upright, and put the tops in the spaces. Cook for approx 30 minutes. Switch off and leave the lid on for a further 10 minutes. Lift out carefully and put the tops back onto the peppers.

NOTE The peppers must be no deeper than 7cm (2½in) to fit in the Remoska.

Timing is the same for the Standard and Grand.

RICE WITH CHICKEN

	Standard	
Serves	2	
Oil	1 tbsp	
Chicken breast, sliced	1	
Spring onion, sliced	3	
Mushrooms, sliced	4 medium	
Water, hot	3 tbsp	
Rice, packet, ready-cooked	1 x 250g	
Nuts, cashew, salted	1 tbsp	

Heat the oil in the Remoska, add the chicken, stir to coat with oil and cook for 10 minutes. Add the onions and mushrooms, cook for further 5–7 minutes. Add the water and the rice. Stir well and cook for 10 minutes or until the rice is heated through. Serve garnished with cashew nuts.

Ready cooked rice in 250g sachets is available in most supermarkets

RICE BAKED WITH HAM

	Standard		Grand	
Serves	4		6–8	
Rice, long grain, cooked	350g	12oz	700g	1¹/₂lb
Eggs, separated	2		4	
Cheese, Cheddar, finely grated	75g	3oz	175g	6oz
Ham, cooked, finely chopped	75g	3oz	175g	6oz
Parsley, fresh, chopped	1 tbsp		2 tbsp	
Tomato purée	¹/₂ tbsp		1 tbsp	
Salt and black pepper				
Oil for brushing				

Leave the cooked rice to go cold. In a bowl mix the rice with the egg yolks, two thirds of the cheese, the ham, parsley, the tomato purée and season. Whisk the egg whites until firm and fold into the rice mix. Brush the Remoska with oil, fill with the rice mixture and cook for approx 30–40 minutes, sprinkle with the rest of the cheese and cook for a further 10 minutes or until the top is pale gold.

Timing is the same for the Standard and Grand.

RICE WITH PEAS & HAM

	Standard		Grand	
Serves	4		8–10	
Rice, easy cook	300g	10oz	500g	1lb
Butter, unsalted	25g	1oz	50g	2oz
Onion, finely chopped	1		2	
Ham, cooked, finely chopped	50g	2oz	100g	4oz
Peas, cooked	200g	7oz	400g	14oz
Cheese, Parmesan, grated	75g	3oz	175g	6oz
Cheese, Cheddar, grated	175g	6oz	300g	10oz
Butter for greasing				

Cook rice according to packet instructions. In a non-stick frying pan fry the onions with the butter until softened and add the ham and peas. Mix with the cooked rice and both the cheeses. Butter the Remoska, fill with the rice mixture and cook for approx 15–20 minutes until crispy and light brown. Serve in wedges.

Timing is the same for the Standard and Grand.

RICE PILAF

Serves	Grand 8	
Butter	75g	3oz
Onion, finely chopped	1 large	
Rice, long grain	350g	12oz
Stock, beef or chicken, warm	700ml	1$^{1}/_{4}$pints
Cinnamon, ground	$^{1}/_{2}$ tsp	
Allspice, ground	$^{1}/_{4}$ tsp	
Cloves, powdered	$^{1}/_{4}$ tsp	
Salt and black pepper		
Pine nuts, pistachio, slivered almonds, mixed	75g	3oz
Currants	50g	2oz

Heat half the butter in the Remoska and cook the onion until soft. Add rice, stir well to coat, cook for 5 minutes. Add the warm stock, cinnamon, allspice, cloves and season, taking into consideration that the stock may already be seasoned. Cook for approx 20 minutes or until all the liquid has been absorbed.

Meanwhile, in a saucepan sauté the nuts and currants in the remaining butter, mix into the rice and serve with lamb or other main dish. Any left over may be mixed with plain yogurt and mayonnaise for a salad.

RICE WITH TUNA & SWEETCORN

Serves	Standard 2	
Tuna in oil, tin	1 x 200g	
Sweetcorn, tin	1 x 180g	
Water, hot	4 tbsp	
Peas, frozen	2 tbsp	
Rice, basmati sachet, ready-cooked	1 x 250g	
Parsley, fresh, chopped	1 tbsp	
Egg, hardboiled	2	

Drain the tins of tuna and sweetcorn, place in the Remoska with the water, stir well and cook for 7–10 minutes. Add the peas and rice, stir and cook for approx 7–10 minutes until heated through and the peas are cooked. Stir in the parsley. Serve garnished with quarters of hard boiled eggs.

NOTE Ready-cooked basmati rice in 250g sachets is available in most supermarkets.

Tagliatelle with Mushroom Sauce

TAGLIATELLE WITH MUSHROOM SAUCE

	Standard		Grand	
Serves	*3–4*		*4–6*	
Oil, olive	1 tbsp		2 tbsp	
Shallots, finely chopped	4		6–8	
Mushrooms, finely sliced	100g	4oz	200g	7oz
Mushroom sauce, jar	1 x 340g		2 x 340g	
Water, warm	150ml	5fl oz	300ml	10fl oz
Pasta, Tagliatelle, fresh	100g	4oz	200g	7oz
Salt and black pepper				

Put the oil, shallots and mushrooms into the Remoska and cook until soft. Add the sauce, fill the empty sauce jar with the water and stir in. Add the tagliatelle, stir to coat with the sauce and cook for approx 15–20 minutes. Season to taste.

Timing is the same for the Standard and Grand.

HEESE

Use your local specialist cheese shops and discover new exciting flavours.

BRIE, BACON & POTATO OMELETTE

	Standard		Grand	
Serves	*4–6*		*6–8*	
Bacon, diced	175g	6oz	225g	8oz
Oil, olive	1 tbsp		2 tbsp	
Spring onions, finely sliced	6–8		8	
Spinach, cooked and drained	175g	6oz	225g	8oz
Potatoes, cooked and sliced	300g	10oz	700g	1¹/2lb
Cheese, Brie or Camembert, sliced	250g	9oz	500g	1lb
Eggs	4		6	
Salt and black pepper				

In a non-stick frying pan cook the bacon until crisp, drain on kitchen paper. Whilst the bacon is cooking, put the oil and spring onions into the Remoska and cook for 15 minutes. Add the bacon, spinach and potatoes, stir lightly to combine. Cover with the cheese slices. Beat the eggs, season to taste, using more freshly ground black pepper than salt and pour over the cheese. Cook for approx 20–25 minutes or until the top is golden. Loosen the edges of the omelette with a spatula and slide onto a warm serving plate.

Timing is the same for the Standard and Grand.

CHEDDAR MUSHROOMS

	Standard		Grand	
Serves	*3–4*		*6–8*	
Spinach, cooked and drained	225g	8oz	350g	12oz
Nutmeg, grated	1/4 tsp		1/2 tsp	
Oil, olive, as needed				
Mushrooms, open cup	6–8 medium		10–12 medium	
Salt and black pepper				
Shallots, finely chopped	2		4	
Cheese, Cheddar, grated	100g	4oz	175g	6oz

Add a generous amount of grated nutmeg to the spinach. Lightly oil the Remoska. Remove the stalks from the mushrooms. Place the mushrooms in a single layer in the Remoska, season with a little salt and plenty of black pepper, drizzle with olive oil. Cook for approx 20 minutes. Remove the mushrooms from the Remoska to a plate lined with kitchen paper. Wipe the Remoska clean. Return the mushrooms to the Remoska. Heat 1 tablespoon of olive oil in a non-stick frying pan and cook the sliced mushroom stalks and shallots until soft and golden. Stir in the spinach, season to taste. Spoon the mixture on top of the mushrooms and cover with cheese. Cook for approx 15–20 minutes, or until the cheese is melted and golden brown. Serve hot as a starter with salad or on toast as a light snack.

Timing is the same for the Standard and Grand.

BRIE & LEEK TART

	Standard or Grand	
Serves	*4*	
Oil, olive	1 tbsp	
Leeks, cleaned and sliced	2	
Shallots, finely sliced	4	
Garlic clove, crushed	1	
Coriander, ground	1/4 tsp	
Salt and black pepper		
Pastry, puff	225g	8oz
Cheese, Brie with garlic and herbs	175g	6oz
Egg	1	
Cream, double	3 tbsp	

Put the oil, leeks, shallots, garlic and coriander in a non-stick frying pan and cook gently until the leeks are soft but not brown, season to taste. Lightly roll out the pastry and line a 20cm (8in) loose bottom tin. Put the cooked vegetables into the pastry case, cover with slices of Brie. Mix together the egg and cream and pour over the Brie. Cook in the Remoska for approx 30–40 minutes or until the top is bubbling and brown.

The same size tart can be cooked in the Grand.

CHEESE TART

	Standard		Grand	
Serves	*4*		*6–8*	
Butter or margarine	50g	2oz	100g	4oz
Lard	25g	1oz	50g	2oz
Flour, plain	100g	4oz	200g	7oz
Cheese, blue	75g	3oz	125g	5oz
Water	1 tbsp		2 tbsp	
Spring onions, chopped	8		12	
Cream, single	200ml	7fl oz	400ml	14fl oz
Eggs	2		3	
Salt and black pepper				

Use the Shallow Pan.

Rub the butter or margarine and lard into the flour until the mixture resembles bread-crumbs or use a food processor. Mix in one third of the cheese and add enough water to bind the pastry. Roll out and line the shallow pan, taking the pastry up the sides to form a rim. Sprinkle the onions on the base of the pastry. Whisk the cream and the eggs together, season to taste and stir in the remaining crumbled blue cheese. Pour into the pastry case. Cook for approx 35–40 minutes until golden brown. Serve warm.

Timing is the same for the Standard and Grand.

COURGETTES STUFFED WITH RICOTTA

	Standard		Grand	
Serves	*4*		*8*	
Breadcrumbs, fresh	25g	1oz	50g	2oz
Milk	2 tbsp		4 tbsp	
Courgettes	4 large		8 large	
Cheese, Ricotta	75g	3oz	175g	6oz
Oregano, dried	1/4 tsp		1/2 tsp	
Egg yolk	1		2	
Salt and black pepper				
Cheese, Parmesan, grated	25g	1oz	50g	2oz

In a bowl, soak the breadcrumbs in the milk. In a saucepan, cook the courgettes whole, in boiling water for 5 minutes. Whilst still warm, cut in half lengthways and scoop out the flesh, taking care not to break the skin. Finely chop the flesh and squeeze out the milk from the breadcrumbs. Mix together the courgette flesh, breadcrumbs, Ricotta, oregano and egg yolk. Season and fill the courgette shells.

Place in a single layer in the Remoska, sprinkle with the cheese and cook for approx 35 minutes.

Timing is the same for the Standard and Grand.

Cheddar, Parsnip and Potato Bake

CHEDDAR, PARSNIP & POTATO BAKE

	Standard		Grand	
Serves	*4–6*		*6–8*	
Potatoes	1kg	2lb	1.3kg	3lb
Parsnips	500g	1lb	700g	1¹/₂lb
Butter as needed				
Salt and black pepper				
Thyme, leaves, fresh	2 tbsp		4 tbsp	
Cream, double	300ml	10fl oz	600ml	20fl oz
Cheese, Cheddar, grated	100g	4oz	225g	8oz

Peel the potatoes and parsnips and cut into chunks, simmer in a saucepan in lightly salted water for 15 minutes, drain and leave until cool enough to handle. Cut into slices. Generously butter the Remoska and layer half the potatoes and parsnips in the Remoska. Season to taste and sprinkle with thyme leaves. Repeat. Pour over the cream and top with the cheese. Cook for approx 40 minutes or until the top is golden.

Timing is the same for the Standard and Grand.

GOAT'S CHEESE FILO PARCELS

	Standard		Grand	
Serves	*4*		*8*	
Relish				
Gooseberries, fresh or frozen	225g	8oz	500g	1lb
Sugar, granulated	50g	2oz	100g	4oz
Water	50ml	2fl oz	100ml	4fl oz
Yogurt, natural	175g	6oz	350g	12oz
Vinegar, Balsamic	1 tsp		2 tsp	
Parcel and filling				
Cheese, goat	175g	6oz	350g	12oz
Herbs, mixed, dried	1 tsp		2 tsp	
Worcestershire sauce	1 tsp		2 tsp	
Black pepper	$1/4$ tsp		$1/2$ tsp	
Egg yolk	1		2	
Pastry, filo, packet	1 x 270g		2 x 270g	
Butter, melted	50g	2oz	100g	4oz

Relish
In a saucepan boil the gooseberries, sugar and water for 8–10 minutes. Pass through a sieve to remove skin and pips. Leave to cool then mix with yogurt and Balsamic vinegar.

Parcel and filling
In a bowl crumble the goat's cheese and mix in the herbs, Worcestershire sauce, black pepper and bind together with the egg yolk. Divide into 8 equal balls for the Standard and 16 for the Grand.

Spread out 3 Filo sheets for the Standard or 6 for the Grand. Brush each with melted butter. Place one sheet on top of the other. Cut into 8 or 16 squares and lay a ball of cheese mixture on each. Brush the edges with melted butter and gather the edges up to form small parcels. Cook in the Remoska for approx 20 minutes until the pastry is pale gold and crispy. Serve with the gooseberry relish.

Timing is the same for the Standard and Grand.

HOT GRUYÈRE & SALMON SANDWICH

	Standard		Grand	
Serves	4		6–8	
Bread, white, slices	6		8	
Butter, softened for spreading				
Salmon trimmings, smoked	200g	7oz	300g	10oz
Cheese, Gruyère, sliced	75g	3oz	100g	4oz

Use the Shallow Pan.

Generously butter each piece of bread. Place half the bread slices butter side down into the Remoska. Cover each slice with the smoked salmon, taking care that it doesn't spill over the edges. Top with the cheese and cover, butter side up, with the remaining bread. Press lightly to seal. Cook for approx 20 minutes or until the bread is golden brown.

Timing is the same for the Standard and Grand.

TOMATOES STUFFED WITH RICOTTA

	Standard		Grand	
Serves	4–6		6–8	
Tomatoes	8–10		12–14	
Salt (see below)				
Stuffing				
Oil, olive	1 tbsp		2 tbsp	
Onion, finely chopped	1 medium		2 medium	
Spinach, cooked, chopped	125g	5oz	200g	7oz
Salt and black pepper				
Nutmeg, fresh, grated	1/4 tsp		1/2 tsp	
Cheese, Ricotta	4 tbsp		6 tbsp	
Egg yolk	1 medium		1 large	
Cheese, Parmesan, grated	4 tbsp		6 tbsp	

Wash and dry the tomatoes and cut off their tops. The number of tomatoes required will depend on the type you choose to use. With the handle of a small teaspoon, scrape out the seeds and partitions, being careful not to pierce the sides of the tomatoes. Lightly salt the cavities and put the tomatoes upside down on kitchen paper to drain.

Stuffing
Heat the oil in a saucepan and gently cook the onions until soft and golden. Remove from the heat. Add the spinach, season to taste with the salt, freshly ground black pepper and nutmeg. Stir in the Ricotta, egg yolk and three-quarters of the Parmesan. Gently blot the tomato cavities with kitchen paper. Fill the cavity with the stuffing. Place the tomatoes in the Remoska, top each with the remaining Parmesan and cook for approx 25-30 minutes. The tomatoes must remain whole. Allow to cool slightly before serving.

Timing is the same for the Standard and Grand.

DES

Substantial, light or delicate, there is plenty of enjoyment in finishing a meal with one of these great recipes.

APPLES WITH HONEY & LEMON

	Standard		Grand	
Serves	*4*		*8*	
Apples, crispy dessert	4		8	
Honey	1 tbsp		3 tbsp	
Lemon, grated zest & juice	1		2	
Butter	25g	1oz	50g	2oz

Core the apples, leaving whole. Cut 4 small slits in the top of each apple and place in the Remoska. Mix the honey, lemon zest, juice and butter together. Spoon the mixture into the centre of the apples and cover with foil. Bake for approx 40 minutes until the apples are tender. Serve with low fat Greek yogurt.

Timing is the same for the Standard and Grand.

APPLE BROWN BETTY

	Standard		Grand	
Serves	*4–6*		*8–10*	
Butter	175g	6oz	300g	10oz
Breadcrumbs, white, fresh	175g	6oz	400g	14oz
Sugar, light soft brown	175g	6oz	300g	10oz
Cinnamon, ground	1 tsp		2 tsp	
Lemon, grated zest and juice	1		3	
Apples, cooking	1kg	2lb	1.3kg	3lb
Water	4 tbsp		8 tbsp	

Butter the Remoska. Melt the butter in a saucepan over a low heat, take off the heat and stir in the breadcrumbs with a fork. In a bowl combine the sugar, cinnamon and the lemon zest. Peel, quarter, core and slice the cooking apples. Sprinkle one third of the buttered crumbs over the base of the Remoska, add a layer of apple slices and cover with half the sugar mixture. Cover with another third of the breadcrumbs, then the rest of the apples and sprinkle over the remainder of the sugar mixture. Finally cover with the rest of the buttered breadcrumbs. Mix the lemon juice with the water and sprinkle over the top. Cover with buttered foil and cook for approx 30–40 minutes, remove the foil and cook for a further 20–30 minutes until the apples are tender and the top is crisp and golden brown. Serve hot with cream.

Timing is the same for the Standard and Grand.

American One Crust Pie

AMERICAN ONE CRUST PIE

	Standard		Grand	
Serves	*4*		*8*	
Pastry, short crust fresh or frozen	300g	10oz	400g	14oz
Egg yolk	1		1	
Semolina	1 tbsp		2 tbsp	
Strawberries, raspberries, blueberries (mixture), fresh	500g	1lb	700g	1¹/₂lb
Sugar, caster	75g	3oz	100g	4oz
Egg white	1		1	
Sugar, granulated	2 tbsp		3 tbsp	

Use the Shallow Pan.

Line the base of the shallow pan with a circle of Magic Non-Stick Liner (see page 12). Roll the pastry out to a round somewhat larger than the base of the Remoska – don't worry if the edges are a little ragged. Roll the pastry round a rolling pin and transfer to the Remoska. Carefully tuck it in around the base and press the rest of the pastry up the sides, do not worry if it is not even. Paint the pastry base with the egg yolk and sprinkle with semolina – this will absorb the juices. Place the fruit in the centre of the pastry, sprinkle with the caster sugar. Turn the pressed up pastry back over the fruit, leaving the centre open, it will look ragged, which is how it should be. Brush the pastry top with the egg white and sprinkle with the granulated sugar. Bake for approx 34–40 minutes or until the crust is golden brown.

Timing is the same for the Standard and Grand.

APPLE & PINE NUT FILO PIE

	Standard		Grand	
Serves	*4*		*6–8*	
Butter	125g	5oz	225g	8oz
Apples, dessert, peeled, cored and sliced	1kg	2lb	1.3kg	3lb
Pine nuts	50g	2oz	75g	3oz
Cinnamon, ground	3 tsp		4 tsp	
Sugar, light soft brown	125g	5oz	225g	8oz
Lemon, grated zest and juice	1		2	
Pastry, filo, packet	1 x 270g		2 x 270g	
Icing sugar to dust				

Melt half of the butter in a large non-stick frying pan over a medium heat. Fry the apples until soft, but not disintegrating. Stir in the pine nuts. Add the cinnamon and after 1 minute the sugar, lemon zest and juice. Let the juices bubble for 5 minutes, stirring continuously. Remove the apples and nuts with a slotted spoon and set aside. Reserve the juices separately.

Melt the remaining butter and brush a little of this on the inside of the Remoska. Lay 2 sheets of pastry inside the Remoska at right angles, with the edges over the sides. Brush the remaining sheets of pastry with the melted butter and continue layering them in the Remoska until all but 2 sheets remain. Spoon the apple mixture in the centre of the pastry, level and fold in all the overlapping edges. Brush the last 2 sheets with butter and cover the apples. Press to seal them in and crinkle the top, pinching the pastry with your fingers. Cook for approx 30 minutes until the top is browned. Dust with icing sugar and serve straight from the Remoska with the reserved juices and ice cream.

Timing is the same for the Standard and Grand.

Milena's Tip

Prevent peeled apples from discolouring by placing them either whole or sliced in water containing the juice of a lemon.

Apple and Orange Plate Pie

APPLE & ORANGE PLATE PIE

	Standard or Grand	
Serves	6	
Pastry		
Flour, plain	225g	8oz
Butter	125g	5oz
Sugar, caster	25g	1oz
Egg yolk	1	
Filling		
Apples, Bramleys	500g	1lb
Orange, grated zest and juice	1	
Sugar, granulated	50g	2oz

Pastry
Rub the flour, butter and sugar together to a fine crumb mixture. Bind together with the egg yolk, cover with clingfilm and chill in the refrigerator for 1 hour.

Filling
Peel and cut up the apples, place in a saucepan, add the orange zest and juice and cook for approximately 15–20 minutes until the apples soften. Add the sugar and cool. This may be done the day before if necessary.

Roll out enough pastry to cover an ovenproof plate which will fit inside the base of the Remoska. Put the pastry onto the plate. Fill with the apple mixture. Roll out the top crust. Wet the edge of the pastry and cover the apples. Trim off the surplus pastry. Pinch up the edges, brush the top with water, make 2 or 3 small slits on the top crust and sprinkle with a little sugar.

Cook in the Remoska for approx 40 minutes.

DANISH APPLE PUDDING

	Standard		Grand	
Serves	*4*		*8*	
Breadcrumbs, fresh, preferably wholemeal	75g	3oz	175g	6oz
Sugar, demerara	50g	2oz	100g	4oz
Hazelnuts, toasted, chopped	50g	2oz	100g	4oz
Apples, cooking, peeled, cored and sliced	500g	1lb	1kg	2lb
Lemon, zest, grated and juice	1		2	
Honey, clear	3 tbsp		6 tbsp	
Egg white	1		2	
Sugar, caster	25g	1oz	50g	2oz

Put the breadcrumbs and demerara sugar in a non-stick frying pan and cook gently for 3–4 minutes, stirring constantly until dark golden, transfer to a bowl and stir in the hazelnuts and set aside. Place the apples, lemon zest and juice in the Remoska, add the honey and cook until the apples are soft, approx 20–30 minutes. Do not be tempted to add any water, the apples will cook beautifully 'fluffy'. Turn out into a bowl and with a wooden spoon beat into a purée. Cool. Whisk the egg white(s) until stiff, whisk in the sugar and fold into the cold apple purée. Spoon half the apple mixture into a bowl, or divide equally into glasses, top with half the breadcrumb mixture, and repeat the layers, finishing with a layer of breadcrumbs and nuts. Serve chilled.

Timing is the same for the Standard and Grand.

APPLE PUDDING

	Standard		Grand	
Serves	*4*		*8*	
Apples, cooking, peeled, cored and sliced	500g	1lb	1kg	2lb
Sugar, demerara	75g	3oz	175g	6oz
Lemon, zest, grated	1		2	
Butter	75g	3oz	200g	7oz
Sugar, caster	75g	3oz	200g	7oz
Eggs	2 small		3 large	
Flour, plain	75g	3oz	175g	6oz
Baking powder	1/2 tsp		1 tsp	

Mix together the apples, demerara sugar and lemon zest. Put in an even layer in the Remoska. Cream the butter and caster sugar thoroughly, add the eggs, a little at a time, beating all the time. Fold in the sieved flour and baking powder. Spread on top of the apples and cook for 35–45 minutes or until the apples are tender and the cake mixture is well risen and firm.

Timing is the same for the Standard and Grand.

BANANAS BAKED WITH APRICOT SAUCE

	Standard	Grand
Serves	*4*	*8*
Aluminium foil pieces	4	8
Bananas, ripe, peeled	4	8
Apricots, tin	1 x 400g	2 x 400g
Sugar	1 tbsp	2 tbsp

Place the foil pieces on a work surface. Place a banana on each one, bring up the sides of the foil to make little packets for the fruit. Purèe the apricots in a blender or processor with a little of the tinned syrup and stir in the sugar. Spoon the purée over the bananas and seal the parcels thoroughly. Cook in the Remoska for approx 20 minutes (open slightly and test with a skewer). Serve hot, letting everyone open their own parcel, which will be full of fruit-scented steam.

Timing is the same for the Standard and Grand.

CHOCOLATE PUDDING

	Standard or Grand	
Serves	4–6	
Butter, unsalted, at room temperature	100g	4oz
Sugar, caster	100g	4oz
Eggs	2	
Vanilla extract	$1/2$ tsp	
Flour, self raising	75g	3oz
Cocoa powder	2 tbsp	
Milk	2 tbsp	
Chocolate Sauce		
Water, hot	300ml	10fl oz
Sugar, soft brown	100g	4oz
Cocoa powder	2 tbsp	

Butter an ovenproof dish, 20cm diameter x 8cm deep (8in diameter x 3in deep). In a large mixing bowl, cream the butter and sugar until pale and light, add the eggs and vanilla extract, and mix together. Sift the flour and cocoa into the bowl, add the milk, and mix until blended. Spoon the mixture into the prepared dish and spread evenly.

Chocolate Sauce
Mix together the water, sugar and cocoa in a jug, and pour over the pudding mixture.

Place the dish in the Standard or the Grand Remoska and bake for approx 35–40 minutes until the top is firm. During cooking the mixture separates, producing a light sponge on top and a chocolate sauce underneath.

Sauce Variation
Substitute 2 tablespoons of the hot water with dark rum.

Milena's Tip

Overripe fruit need not be thrown away. Purée it with some caster sugar and a little lemon juice to make a sauce. Serve with ice cream or yogurt.

DRIED FRUIT & NUT TART

	Standard or Grand		
Serves	6		
Pastry			
Pastry, ready made to line a 20cm (8in) flan tin			
Filling			
Cream, double	250ml	8fl oz	
Eggs, beaten	4		
Nuts, mixed	100g	4oz	
Pine nuts, toasted	100g	4oz	
Almonds, flaked	100g	4oz	
Raisins	100g	4oz	
Sugar	175g	6oz	
Vanilla essence	$^1/_2$ tsp		
Icing sugar for dusting	25g	1oz	

Roll out the pastry to fit into the flan tin.

Filling
In a bowl, stir the cream into the eggs and add the other ingredients except the icing sugar. Mix well and spread into the flan case. Cook in the Remoska for approx 35–40 minutes. When cooked, cool slightly and sprinkle with icing sugar.

May be cooked in either the Standard or the Grand.

EGG CUSTARD

	Standard or Grand		
Serves	4		
Milk, whole or semi-skimmed	500ml	1pint	
Sugar, caster	75g	3oz	
Vanilla, split pod or extract			
Lemon, sliver of zest			
Eggs	3 whole and 2 yolks		

Grease a 1litre (2pt) ovenproof dish. Put the milk in a saucepan with the sugar, vanilla pod or a few drops of vanilla extract and lemon zest. Bring just to the boil, cover and remove from the heat for 10 minutes for the flavours to infuse.

Whisk the eggs and yolks together, add the warm milk, whisking all the time. Strain the custard mixture into the ovenproof dish. Place the dish into the Remoska. Make a bain-marie by pouring enough cold water around the dish, until it almost reaches the top of the dish. Cook for 55–60 minutes (topping up with cold water during the cooking as necessary) until firm and a knife tip in the centre comes out clean.

NECTARINE PUFFS

	Standard		Grand	
Serves	*4*		*8*	
Nectarines	4		8	
Pastry, puff	250g	9oz	500g	1lb
Marzipan	50g	2oz	100g	4oz
Walnut halves	8		16	

Halve and stone the nectarines. Roll out the pastry to $^1/_2$cm ($^1/_4$in) thick. Cut out circles with a 7cm (3in) cutter. Divide the marzipan into 8 pieces for the Standard and 16 for the Grand and place a piece in the centre of each circle of pastry. Place a walnut half on top of each, then place a half nectarine cut side down on top of each. Cook in the Remoska for approx 20–30 minutes.

Allow to cool slightly and remove the skin. Sprinkle lightly with demerara sugar and return to the Remoska for a further 5 minutes or until the sugar melts over the top. Eat hot or cold.

Timing is the same for the Standard and Grand.

PANETTONE BREAD PUDDING WITH FRUIT

	Standard		Grand	
Serves	*4*		*8*	
Fruit, dried, mixed	75g	3oz	175g	6oz
Apple juice	150ml	5fl oz	300ml	10fl oz
Panettone, diced	175g	6oz	350g	12oz
Cinnamon, ground	1 tsp		2 tsp	
Banana, large, sliced	1		2	
Panettone, sliced	4 slices		6–8 slices	
Egg yolk	1		2	
Milk, semi-skimmed	150ml	5fl oz	300ml	10fl oz
Sugar, demerara	1 tbsp		2 tbsp	

Place the dried fruit in a saucepan with the apple juice and bring to the boil. Remove the pan from the heat and stir in the diced Panettone, cinnamon and banana. Transfer the mixture into the Remoska. Cut the extra slices of Panettone into triangles and arrange on top, overlapping slightly. Whisk the egg yolk and milk together and pour through a sieve over the prepared pudding. Leave to soak for 20 minutes. Sprinkle with sugar and cook for approx 25–35 minutes until firm and golden brown. Serve hot or cold with yogurt.

Timing is the same for the Standard and Grand.

PEACHES STUFFED WITH CHOCOLATE

	Standard		Grand	
Serves	*4*		*8*	
Peaches	4		8	
Almonds, chopped	50g	2oz	100g	4oz
Macaroon biscuits, crushed	6		12	
Chocolate, bitter, grated	50g	2oz	100g	4oz
Butter	as needed		as needed	
Wine, white, sweet	300ml	10fl oz	600ml	20fl oz
Sugar	100g	4oz	200g	7oz

Halve and stone the peaches. Remove a little of the pulp from each half and combine with the almonds, macaroons and chocolate and mix well. If a little dry, add a little of the wine. Fill each peach half with the mixture and top with a little knob of butter. Place into the Remoska, pour in the wine, add the sugar. Cook for approx 30–40 minutes and serve hot.

Timing is the same for the Standard and Grand.

PEACHES STUFFED WITH MACAROON BISCUITS

	Standard		Grand	
Serves	*4*		*8*	
Peaches, firm	4 large		8 large	
Amaretto or macaroon biscuits	75g	3oz	175g	6oz
Sugar, caster	50g	2oz	100g	4oz
Amaretto liquor	1 tbsp		3 tbsp	
Egg yolk	1		2	
Lemon, zest, grated	1/2		1	
Almonds, flaked	25g	1oz	75g	3oz

Halve and stone the peaches. Scoop a little flesh from the centre of each half. Add the crushed biscuits and mix with the remaining ingredients except the almonds. Beat until smooth. Fill the peach halves and sprinkle with the flaked almonds. Cook in the Remoska for approx 20–30 minutes, serve warm or cold with ice cream or double cream.

Timing is the same for the Standard and Grand.

PEAR AND ORANGE CAKE WITH WALNUT TOPPING

	Standard or Grand	
Serves	*4–6*	
Butter, softened	100g	4oz
Sugar, soft brown	125g	5oz
Eggs	2	
Flour, plain	250g	9oz
Baking powder	3 tsp	
Orange juice, fresh	2 tbsp	
Orange, zest, grated	2 tsp	
Vanilla essence, few drops		
Pears, cored and chopped	500g	1lb
Cake tin liner available from Lakeland		
Topping		
Butter	25g	1oz
Flour, plain	50g	2oz
Sugar, brown	2 tbsp	
Cinnamon, ground	2 tsp	
Walnuts, chopped	1 tbsp	

Beat the butter with the sugar until pale and fluffy. Beat in the eggs. Sift the flour with the baking powder and fold in with the orange juice, zest and vanilla essence. Stir in the pear chunks. Place the cake liner into the Remoska and turn the cake mixture into the liner. Level the surface.

Topping
Rub the butter into the flour until it resembles breadcrumbs. Mix in the sugar, cinnamon and walnuts. Sprinkle over the cake.

Cook for approx 55 minutes, then turn out and peel off the liner. Place the cake, base side down on a wire rack to cool.

Milena's Tip

If brown sugar has hardened in the store cupboard wrap the pack in a damp tea towel and microwave on Medium for a minute or two. The sugar will begin to soften.

PLUM BREAD PUDDING

	Standard		Grand	
Serves	4		8–10	
Bread, white, day old, cubed	100g	4oz	400g	14oz
Milk	75ml	3fl oz	150ml	5fl oz
Butter	60g	2^1/$_2$oz	125g	5oz
Sugar, icing	50g	2oz	120g	4^1/$_2$oz
Cheese, curd	250g	9oz	500g	1lb
Egg yolks	2		5	
Raisins	50g	2oz	75g	3oz
Brandy (optional)	1 tbsp		3 tbsp	
Sugar, vanilla	1 tsp		3 tsp	
Plums, stoned, sliced	225g	8oz	500g	1lb
Egg whites	2		5	

Place the bread in a bowl, sprinkle the milk over it to 'dampen it', gently stir it around. Cream the butter and sugar, add the curd cheese, the egg yolks, raisins (soaked overnight in the brandy) and the vanilla sugar. Cut the plum slices into small cubes and add to the creamed mix. Stir in the bread cubes, whisk the egg whites until stiff and fold into the mixture. Lightly grease the Remoska and fill with the plum mix. Smooth to level and cover with a piece of greaseproof paper cut to fit the circumference, or use a Magic Non-Stick Liner (see page 12). Cook for approx 35–45 minutes. The mix will rise like a soufflé.

After the designated time take a look. Remove the greaseproof paper or liner. If the edges are cooking faster than the centre simply cut a hole in the centre of the paper/liner the diameter of a tea cup. Replace the paper/liner and carry on cooking until the surface is pale gold and well risen. Serve warm.

Timing is the same for the Standard and Grand.

Milena's Tip

To get more juice out of a lemon, wrap it in kitchen towel and place in the microwave for 10 seconds on full power.

PLUMS BAKED IN WINE

	Standard		Grand	
Serves	*4*		*6–8*	
Plums, firm	1kg	2lb	1.5kg	3lb
Sugar, demerara	175g	6oz	400g	14oz
Port wine	75ml	3fl oz	250ml	8fl oz
Water	75ml	3fl oz	175ml	6fl oz

Put the plums in the Remoska. Sprinkle with sugar. Add the port wine and water and cook for approx 35 minutes. The plums should retain their shape. Serve hot or cold with thick custard, ice cream or slightly whipped double cream.

Timing is the same for the Standard and Grand.

PLUM CHARLOTTE

	Standard		Grand	
Serves	*4–6*		*8–10*	
Butter	50g	2oz	100g	4oz
Breadcrumbs, fresh, white	175g	6oz	400g	14oz
Plums, ripe	700g	1^1/2lb	1.5kg	3lb
Sugar, soft brown	100g	4oz	300g	10oz
Lemon, grated zest and juice	^{1}/2		1	
Orange juice, fresh	200ml	7fl oz	400ml	14fl oz

Grease the base and sides of the Remoska. Cover the base with one third of the breadcrumbs. Halve and stone the plums. Place a layer of plums on top of the breadcrumbs and sprinkle with half of the sugar, lemon zest and juice. Dot with butter. Continue with another layer, finishing with a layer of breadcrumbs and dot with butter. Pour over the orange juice and cook for approx 40 minutes or until the Charlotte feels tender when pierced with a skewer, and the top is golden brown. Serve straight from the Remoska. Good with custard.

Timing is the same for the Standard and Grand.

PLUM COMPOTE

	Standard		Grand	
Serves	4		6–8	
Wine, red or port	1 glass		3 glasses	
Redcurrant jelly	4 tbsp		8 tbsp	
Orange, grated zest and juice	1		3	
Plums, red	500g	1lb	1.5kg	3lb

Pour the wine into a saucepan and reduce by half. Add the redcurrant jelly, stir to melt, add the orange zest and juice. Transfer to the Remoska. Halve and stone the plums, place rounded side down in the sauce and cook until the fruit is tender, approx 20–30 minutes. Cool and serve with ice cream or whipped double cream.

Timing is the same for the Standard and Grand.

PLUM CRUMBLE

	Standard		Grand	
Serves	4–6		8–10	
Plums	6–8		10–12	
Sugar (see below)				
Crumble				
Flour, plain	500g	1lb	700g	1^1/2lb
Butter	225g	8oz	400g	14oz
Sugar	100g	4oz	200g	7oz
Cinnamon, ground	2 tsp		3 tsp	

Halve and stone enough plums to fit tightly into the base of the Remoska. Cook until the plums are slightly softened. Sprinkle with sugar.

Crumble
Rub together or process the crumble mix and sprinkle thickly over the top. Cook until the crumble is light brown, approx 30–40 minutes. Serve hot with ice cream.

Timing is the same for Standard and Grand.

Milena's Tip

Quick hot pancake pudding.
Layer six pancakes with different jams, place in the Remoska, drizzle with a little melted butter and maple syrup. Heat for about 5 minutes until hot. Serve with ice cream.

RHUBARB CRUMBLE

	Standard		Grand	
Serves	*4*		*6–8*	
Crumble mixture				
Flour, plain	100g	4oz	200g	7oz
Oats, rolled	50g	2oz	100g	4oz
Margarine, vegetable	50g	2oz	100g	4oz
Sugar, demerara	50g	2oz	100g	4oz
Cinnamon, ground	1/2 tsp		1 tsp	
Rhubarb	700g	11/2lb	1.5kg	3lb
Stem ginger, preserved	1 piece		2 pieces	
Honey	1 tbsp		3 tbsp	
Water	1 tbsp		4 tbsp	

Place the flour and oats in a bowl and rub in the margarine to a fine consistency, stir in the sugar and cinnamon – or whiz all in a food processor. Trim the rhubarb. Cut into 1cm (1/2in) lengths. Place the rhubarb in the Remoska, sprinkle in the diced ginger, drizzle with honey and water and top with the crumble mixture. Cook for approx 20–30 minutes until the fruit is soft and the topping golden brown. Serve hot or cold with natural yogurt.

Timing is the same for the Standard and Grand.

RICE PUDDING

	Standard		Grand	
Serves	*4*		*8*	
Rice, Arborio	50g	2oz	100g	4oz
Sugar	25g	1oz	50g	2oz
Milk, full cream	600ml	20fl oz	1l	32fl oz
Cream, double (optional)	2 tbsp		2 tbsp	
Nutmeg, fresh, grated				

Place the rice in the Remoska, cover with boiling water and leave for 10 minutes. Strain off the water, stir in the sugar, milk and cream (if using). Sprinkle with nutmeg. Cook for approx 1–11/2 hours, until thick and creamy, stirring occasionally. If it is cooking too quickly, cover with foil.

Timing is the same for the Standard and Grand.

SUMMER FRUITS COBBLER

	Standard		Grand	
Serves	4		6–8	
Rhubarb	350g	12oz	700g	1^1/$_2$lb
Sugar (see below)				
Strawberries, fresh	225g	8oz	500g	1lb
Raspberries, fresh	100g	4oz	250g	9oz
Blueberries, fresh	100g	4oz	250g	9oz
Scones				
Flour, self-raising	350g	12oz	500g	1lb
Baking powder	15g	^{1}/$_2$oz	20g	^{3}/$_4$oz
Sugar	50g	2oz	75g	3oz
Butter or margarine	75g	3oz	100g	4oz
Milk	50ml	2fl oz	75ml	3fl oz

Cut the rhubarb into 2^1/$_2$cm (2in) lengths, add sugar to taste and cook in the Remoska for approx 10–15 minutes, until soft. Add the other fruits. While the fruit is cooking make the scones.

Scones
Sieve the flour and baking powder together and add the sugar. Rub in the butter to a fine crumb mixture. Mix in the milk to a soft dough. You may need more or less milk depending on the flour. Roll out on a floured surface to a 2^1/$_2$cm (2in) thickness. Cut out circles with a 5cm (2^1/$_2$in) cutter. Place overlapping on top of the fruit. Brush with a little milk and cook for approx 15–20 minutes.

RICOTTA CHEESE CAKE

	Standard	
Serves	6	
Cheese, Ricotta	500g	1lb
Egg yolks	2	
Sugar, caster	100g	4oz
Candied peel	25g	1oz
Brandy or rum	150ml	5fl oz
Lemon, zest, grated	1	
Salt	^{1}/$_4$ tsp	
Butter for greasing		
Breadcrumbs, dried	1 tbsp	
Cinnamon, ground and caster sugar, mixed	1 tsp	

Sieve the Ricotta into a bowl; add the whisked egg yolks, sugar, candied peel, brandy or rum, lemon zest and salt. Grease the base of the Remoska. Sprinkle the base with breadcrumbs, place the cheese mixture into the Remoska and cook for approx 30–35 minutes until set. Sprinkle with the cinnamon/sugar mix and serve warm or cold.

B

AKING

Practice, patience and enthusiasm are the key to confident and successful baking, bringing satisfaction to the baker and those lucky enough to enjoy the results!

ALMOND CAKE

	Standard or Grand	
Serves	6	
Oil for greasing		
Butter	100g	4oz
Sugar	125g	5oz
Eggs	3	
Almonds, ground	75g	3oz
Almond essence	2–3 drops	
Flour, plain	40g	1^1/$_2$oz
Sugar, caster, for dusting		

Grease the Remoska with a little oil. Soften the butter and add the sugar, beat until soft and light. Add the eggs, one at a time, adding one third of the ground almonds with each egg. Beat well. Mix in the essence and fold in the flour. Cook for approx 40 minutes. Dust the top with caster sugar.

If using the Grand Remoska place the mixture into a 20cm (8in) cake tin.

Milena's Tip

Place a few sugar cubes in your biscuit tin to help keep biscuits crisp and fresh. Did you know the sugar cube was a Czech invention of 1843 in a town called Dacice.

Chocolate Cake from Vienna

CHOCOLATE CAKE FROM VIENNA

	Grand	
Serves	*8–10*	
Springform cake tin, 25cm (10in)		
Chocolate, dark, 70%	180g	6^{1}/$_{2}$oz
Butter, softened	175g	6oz
Sugar, caster	125g	5oz
Eggs, separated	4	
Almonds, ground	200g	7oz
Icing		
Jam, apricot, heated and sieved	5 tbsp	
Chocolate, dark, 70%	100g	4oz
Butter	25g	1oz

Line the cake tin with baking parchment and lightly grease with butter. Break the chocolate into pieces and melt in a microwave or over a pan of simmering hot water. Cream together the butter and three quarters of the sugar, add the egg yolks, ground almonds and the melted chocolate and whisk well. Whisk the egg whites until stiff and whisk in the rest of the sugar. Fold in stages into the chocolate mixture using a metal spoon. Pour into the prepared cake tin, place in the Remoska (line the base of the Remoska with a Magic Non-Stick Liner (see page 12) before putting the cake tin in – it prevents the non-stick base from getting scratched) and cook for approx 35–40 minutes.

After 25–30 minutes, cover the top of the cake with a wide ring of Magic Liner to prevent the edges from overcooking, whilst the centre continues to cook. Test with a wooden 'kebab' stick. The centre will be a little 'sticky' when cut. Remove from the Remoska, run a knife round the cake and take out of the tin. Leave to cool.

Brush the top with the jam. Cool. Melt the chocolate and stir in the butter. Pour over the cake and smooth across the top. Leave to set.

IRISH SODA BREAD

	Standard or Grand	
Flour, plain	225g	8oz
Flour, wholemeal	225g	8oz
Salt	1 tsp	
Bicarbonate of soda	2 tsp	
Cream of tartar	2 tsp	
Butter or lard	40g	1^{1}/$_{2}$oz
Sugar, caster	1 tsp	
Milk	350ml	12fl oz

Sieve the flours and salt into a large bowl. Add the bicarbonate of soda and cream of tartar, rub into the butter or lard. Stir in the sugar. Pour in sufficient milk (you may need more depending on the flour) to mix to a soft dough. Do not overmix or the bread will be heavy and tough. Shape into a round on a lightly floured surface. Place a small bowl of water in the Remoska and heat for 4 minutes. Cut a deep cross in the top of the dough and dust lightly with wholemeal flour. Remove the bowl of water, place the dough in the Remoska and cook for approx 35-40 minutes or until well risen and the bread sounds hollow when tapped on the base. Best served warm.

For the Grand, double the ingredients and make two loaves to fit the pan. Cook approx 40-45 minutes.

MINCE TARTS

	Standard or Grand	
Flour, plain	175g	6oz
Butter	125g	5oz
Egg, yolk	1	
Cream, double	1 tbsp	
Brandy	1 tbsp	
Mincemeat, as required		
Icing sugar, as required		
Small tin foil cases		

Lightly rub the sieved flour and the chilled butter together to a fine crumb stage. Mix together the egg yolk, cream and brandy. Add to the crumb mixture to form a pastry, do not over mix. Chill in the refrigerator for 1 hour. Roll out thinly, this is best done a small amount at a time as the pastry is so rich it may be difficult to handle. With a 6cm (2^{1}/$_{2}$in) cutter cut out circles and place into tin foil cases. Fill with 2 teaspoons of your favourite mincemeat. Roll out more pastry and cut smaller circles for the tops.

This should make 16–20 tarts. Place a number of them in the Remoska and cook for approx 10–15 minutes until golden. Remove, cool slightly and dust with icing sugar.

May be cooked in either the Standard or Grand.

ECCLES CAKES

	Standard or Grand	
Currants	500g	1lb
Sugar, caster	75g	3oz
Butter	75g	3oz
Nutmeg, fresh, grated	$1/4$ tsp	
Pastry, puff	350g	12oz

Mix the currants, sugar, butter and nutmeg together. Cut the pastry into approx 25g (1oz) pieces and roll out. Place 1 heaped tablespoon of the currant mix on the centre, gather in the edges to make a small purse and gently roll into a circle. Brush with water. Place more sugar onto a flat plate and dip the wet top of the Eccles cake in it. Lightly score the top. Place in the Remoska and cook for approx 10–15 minutes until light gold.

May be cooked in either the Standard or Grand.

REDCURRANT & BLACKBERRY CAKE

	Standard		Grand	
Serves	*4–6*		*8–10*	
Flour, self raising	100g	4oz	175g	6oz
Sugar, caster	50g	2oz	75g	3oz
Egg	1 small		1 large	
Cheese, curd	1 tbsp		2 tbsp	
Butter, melted	50g	2oz	75g	3oz
Milk	1 tbsp		2 tbsp	
Redcurrants, fresh	75g	3oz	125g	5oz
Blackberries, fresh	75g	3oz	125g	5oz
Sugar, icing				

Use the Shallow Pan.

Sift the flour into a bowl, add the sugar, egg, cheese and butter, mix to a sticky dough and thin it with a little milk. Stir in the fruits. Line the shallow pan with a circle of Magic Non-Stick Liner (see page 12). Spoon the mixture into the pan, flour your fingers and the palm of your hand and gently press the dough evenly to make a round flat cake. This is a sticky dough and cannot be rolled out. Cook for approx 30–40 minutes or until cake is risen and pale gold in colour. Leave to cool for a few minutes. Place a plate over the pan and turn the cake out, peel off the liner and turn the cake again using a cooling cake rack. Dust with icing sugar before serving.

Timing is the same for the Standard and Grand.

Milena's Tip

To stop pastry shells from going soggy, brush the inside with some beaten egg white whilst the pastry is hot. It will harden and form a seal.

SCONES

	Standard		Grand	
Flour, plain	225g	8oz	450g	15oz
Baking powder	1 tsp		2 tsp	
Margarine	50g	2oz	100g	4oz
Sugar	40g	1¹/₂oz	75g	3oz
Sultanas	40g	1¹/₂oz	75g	3oz
Egg	¹/₂		1	
Milk	100ml	4fl oz	200ml	7fl oz

Sieve together the flour and baking powder. Rub in the margarine, add the sugar and sultanas. Whisk the egg and milk together, make a hollow in the flour and pour the liquid in, saving a small amount for brushing the tops. Mix lightly and roll out to approx 2cm (1in) thickness. Cut out with a 6cm (2¹/₂in) cutter, brush the scones with the remaining milk/egg mix. Place in the Remoska and cook for approx 15–20 minutes to pale gold. Best served warm, sandwiched with whipped cream and jam.

SAUCES

Sauces need to be made

in a separate saucepan.

APPLE SAUCE

Apples, Bramleys	500g	1lb
Lemon, zest and juice	1	
Sugar, caster	1 tbsp	
Butter	15g	$1/2$oz

Most sauces need to be stirred during the cooking so the Remoska is not practical, except for apple sauce for which it is perfect. Peel and core the apples. Pare the lemon zest very thinly. Place the apples, the zest and juice of lemon in the Remoska. Do not be tempted to add any water. Cook for approx 10 minutes – you need to keep your eye on this. The apples will 'fluff' up into a very soft pulp. Beat with a wooden spoon until smooth or put through a strainer. Stir in the sugar and butter.

BÉCHAMEL SAUCE

Onion	1 small	
Cloves	2	
Bay leaf	1	
Thyme, fresh, sprigs	2	
Rosemary, fresh, sprig	1	
Peppercorns	6	
Parsley stalks	4	
Milk, hot	600ml	20fl oz
Butter, unsalted	75g	3oz
Flour, plain	75g	3oz
Salt and white pepper		
Cream, double (optional)	1–2 tbsp	

A good Béchamel sauce is worth a little trouble and the herb ingredients make all the difference. This is a major sauce which forms the base for many others. The milk is infused with herbs to give a delicate and subtle flavour, unlike an ordinary white sauce. It may be used as a base for mornay (cheese), soubise (onion), mushroom or egg sauces.

Stud the onion with the cloves and together with the bay leaf, thyme, rosemary, peppercorns and the parsley stalks, infuse in hot milk. Leave to rest for 15 minutes, strain the milk and leave to cool. In a saucepan melt the butter, add the sieved flour and stir well with a wooden spoon until the mixture turns into a fine crumb texture. Gradually add the milk and bring to the boil, stirring constantly. Adjust the seasoning and simmer gently for a further 12–15 minutes. Add, if you wish 2 tablespoons of double cream.

BREAD SAUCE

Onion	1 small	
Mace	1 blade	
Peppercorns, white	6	
Milk	300ml	10fl oz
Breadcrumbs, white, fresh	50g	2oz
Salt to taste		
Butter	25g	1oz
Cream, double	1 tbsp	

Simmer the onion, mace and peppercorns in the milk for approx 20 minutes. Strain, add the breadcrumbs and season. Simmer gently until the consistency is similar to thick cream. Add the butter and cream. Re-heat to serve.

BASIC INGREDIENTS FOR GOOD GRAVY

Oil	1 tbsp
Caraway seed	2 tsp
Onion, carrot, leek, roughly chopped	2 tbsp
Turnip, parsnip, mushrooms, roughly chopped	1 tbsp
Salt and black pepper	

Heat the oil in a non-stick frying pan, add the caraway seed and all chopped ingredients. Season, stir and leave to cook for approx 20 minutes. Stir and cook for a further 10 minutes, transfer the mix to your Remoska. Place your chosen meat on top, add the required water or stock and carry on cooking according to the recipe. When the meat is cooked, remove from the Remoska and keep warm. Tip the rest of the vegetables and juices into a jug and skim off the fat. Liquidise, if too thick add water or meat stock.

BASIC MARINADE FOR GAME

Oil, good olive	4 tbsp
Wine, red or dry sherry	2 tbsp
Lemon zest, grated	1 tsp
Nutmeg, fresh grated	to taste
Juniper berries, crushed	1 tbsp
Garlic clove, crushed	1
Salt and black pepper	

Combine all ingredients and whisk well or shake in a screw-top jar. The marinade will keep in the refrigerator for 2–3 weeks.

CHEESE SAUCE

Make a Béchamel sauce (see page 180) and add 100g (4oz) grated cheese whilst still warm. Mix well to a smooth sauce, add 1 level teaspoonful of English or French mustard.

CHOCOLATE SAUCE

Sugar, caster	50g	2oz
Water	150ml	5fl oz
Coffee, instant	1/2 tsp	
Chocolate, plain 70%	50g	2oz
Vanilla essence or brandy or rum	1 tsp	
Cream, double (optional)		

Dissolve the sugar in the water and bring to the boil. Lower the heat and add the coffee powder and the broken chocolate. When the chocolate is thoroughly melted, bring to the boil. Simmer for 5 minutes. Stir in the vanilla essence or the brandy or rum. Stir in the cream if used. Serve hot or cold.

MOUSSELINE SAUCE

Egg yolks	2	
Butter	75g	3oz
Lemon, juice	1/2 a lemon	
Salt and white pepper		
Cream, double	4 tbsp	

Put the yolks into a bowl, add 1 tsp of the butter and stand the bowl in a small saucepan of simmering water. Whisk until the mixture is thick, then add the lemon juice and season lightly. Keep whisking and gradually add the remaining butter (slightly softened). When the sauce is thick remove from the heat and continue to whisk for 1–2 minutes. Lightly whip the cream and fold into the sauce.

Serve with asparagus or salmon.

MINT SAUCE

Mint, fresh	3 tbsp
Sugar, caster	1 tbsp
Water, boiling	2 tbsp
Vinegar, wine, white	to taste

Chop the washed mint and pound with the caster sugar until quite smooth. Add 1–2 tablespoons of boiling water, according to the quantity of mint, to improve the colour and melt the sugar. Add wine vinegar to taste.

MUSHROOM SAUCE

Garlic cloves, crushed	2	
Onion, chopped	1	
Oil, olive	2 tbsp	
Mushrooms, sliced	225g	8oz
Tomatoes	500g	1lb
Marjoram, dried	1/2 tsp	
Salt and black pepper		
Stock, mushroom	175ml	6fl oz
Parsley, fresh, chopped	see below	
Soured cream (optional)	1 tbsp	

Fry the garlic and onion in the oil until soft, add the mushrooms and fry until they release juice. Stir in scalded, peeled and chopped tomatoes, add the marjoram, season and continue to cook a further 5 minutes. Add the stock and simmer for a further 10 minutes. Liquidise, add a handful of parsley. Stir in the soured cream if required.

MUSTARD SAUCE

Butter	100g	4oz
Mustard, French or German	6 tbsp	
Cream, double	150ml	5fl oz
Flour, plain	1 tbsp	
Parsley, fresh, chopped	4 tbsp	
Paprika, sweet	$1/2$ tsp	

Melt the butter in a saucepan on a low heat and add the mustard, stirring constantly. Do not let it boil, it will separate. Stir in the cream, sifted flour, parsley, sweet paprika and simmer just enough to cook the flour and until the sauce thickens.

ONION SAUCE

Onions, sliced	2 large	
Butter	25g	1oz
Béchamel sauce	300ml	10fl oz
Cream, double (optional)	1 tbsp	
Salt and white pepper		

In a saucepan, blanch the onions by putting in cold water, bringing to the boil and draining. Melt the butter in a saucepan, add the onion and cook covered until tender but not coloured. Remove from the pan and purée in a blender. Add the purée to the hot Béchamel sauce (see page 180), stir in the cream (if using) and season the sauce well.

PEPPER SAUCE

Onion, finely chopped	1 large	
Oil, olive	2 tbsp	
Peppers, green	2 large	
Peppers, red	2 large	
Tomatoes	500g	1lb
Sugar, caster	1 tsp	
Vinegar, wine, red	50ml	2fl oz
Salt and black pepper		
Parsley, fresh, chopped	4 tbsp	

Fry the onions in the oil until soft, add the finely chopped peppers and continue to gently fry for a further 5 minutes. Stir in scalded, peeled and chopped tomatoes, add the sugar, vinegar, seasoning and simmer slowly until thickened. Finally stir in the parsley. Cool and store in a jar in the refrigerator. Shake before using. Good poured over hard-boiled eggs or cold cooked leeks.

TOMATO SAUCE

Garlic cloves, crushed	2	
Oil, olive	2 tbsp	
Tomatoes, ripe	500g	1lb
Sugar, caster	1 tbsp	
Oregano or marjoram, dried	1 tsp	
Salt and black pepper		
Parsley, fresh, chopped	2 tbsp	

Fry the garlic in the oil, add scalded, peeled and chopped tomatoes, sugar, oregano or marjoram, season and cook until the tomatoes are tender. Liquidise, finally stir in the chopped parsley.

INDEX

Soup   15

Vegetables   23

Pasta and Rice — 137

Cheese — 145

Desserts — 153

REMOSKA®
COOKING

200 RECIPES
FOR THE STANDARD & GRAND REMOSKA®

Milena Grenfell-Baines

published by

Hooray for Home Cooking Limited

First published in 2007
Reprinted 2007
Reprinted 2008

Hooray for Home Cooking Limited
PO Box 456
Preston Central
Preston
Lancashire
PR1 8GG

British Library Cataloguing in Publication Data.
A catalogue record for this book is available from the British Library.

ISBN No 978-0-9544900-1-0

Recipes by
Milena Grenfell-Baines
Derek Smith
Joan Whittle
Jill Wadeson

Design
Gradwell Corporate Design

Photography
Fourninety

Photographer
Sharon Crowley

Art Direction
Lanie Green

Food Stylist
Andi Wright

Editor
Milena Grenfell Baines

Assistant Editor
Jill Wadeson

Pre-press by
Lancashire Printing Company Limited

Printed in China through Phoenix Offset